1,000,000 Books

are available to read at

Forgotten Books

www.ForgottenBooks.com

Read online
Download PDF
Purchase in print

ISBN 978-0-282-58159-6
PIBN 10857787

This book is a reproduction of an important historical work. Forgotten Books uses state-of-the-art technology to digitally reconstruct the work, preserving the original format whilst repairing imperfections present in the aged copy. In rare cases, an imperfection in the original, such as a blemish or missing page, may be replicated in our edition. We do, however, repair the vast majority of imperfections successfully; any imperfections that remain are intentionally left to preserve the state of such historical works.

Forgotten Books is a registered trademark of FB &c Ltd.
Copyright © 2018 FB &c Ltd.
FB &c Ltd, Dalton House, 60 Windsor Avenue, London, SW19 2RR.
Company number 08720141. Registered in England and Wales.

For support please visit www.forgottenbooks.com

1 MONTH OF FREE READING

at

www.ForgottenBooks.com

By purchasing this book you are eligible for one month membership to ForgottenBooks.com, giving you unlimited access to our entire collection of over 1,000,000 titles via our web site and mobile apps.

To claim your free month visit: www.forgottenbooks.com/free857787

* Offer is valid for 45 days from date of purchase. Terms and conditions apply.

English
Français
Deutsche
Italiano
Español
Português

www.forgottenbooks.com

Mythology Photography **Fiction**
Fishing Christianity **Art** Cooking
Essays Buddhism Freemasonry
Medicine **Biology** Music **Ancient Egypt** Evolution Carpentry Physics
Dance Geology **Mathematics** Fitness
Shakespeare **Folklore** Yoga Marketing
Confidence Immortality Biographies
Poetry **Psychology** Witchcraft
Electronics Chemistry History **Law**
Accounting **Philosophy** Anthropology
Alchemy Drama Quantum Mechanics
Atheism Sexual Health **Ancient History**
Entrepreneurship Languages Sport
Paleontology Needlework Islam
Metaphysics Investment Archaeology
Parenting Statistics Criminology
Motivational

Have You tried?

BUCHANAN'S

Home=Made

Delicious

MARMALADE,

JAMS & JELLIES,

CHOCOLATES,

SPECIALITIES
J. B. B. Mints
Royal Toffee
Butter Scotch

CONFECTIONERY

JOHN BUCHANAN & BROS., Ld., GLASGOW.

ADVERTISEMENTS.

The Pure Home=made Cocoa.

MAZAWATTEE COCOA

is a sterling British product composed solely of the finest Cocoa beans, and is prepared by greatly improved methods.

ESTABLISHED 1848.

THOS. HART,

Saddler,

 BALFRON.

Supplies all Kinds of HARNESS and STABLE REQUISITES at Reasonable Prices.

ORDERS PUNCTUALLY ATTENDED TO.

ADVERTISEMENTS.

PICTURES

"A room without Pictures is like a house without .. windows."

—*Ruskin.*

A Collection of tastefully Framed ETCHINGS always in Stock, by the most Famous Artistes, including Joseph Israels, Meissonier, M'Whirter, Peter Graham, and many others. Our Stock of OIL PAINTINGS is large, and comprises attractive works by well-known Artistes at specially Low Prices.

For the convenience of Customers residing in the Country, a PORTFOLIO of ETCHINGS can be sent for Selection at any time.

Buyers waited on by Appointment.

PICTURE FRAMING A SPECIALITY.

DAVIDSON, KAY & CO.,
FINE ART DEALERS,
87 and 89 LONDON STREET, GLASGOW.

ESTABLISHED 1859.   NATIONAL TELEPHONE, 67Y1.

HIGH-CLASS TEAS.

TEA IS OUR SPECIALITY.

In our Teas the Public realise every advantage in Price, with absolute uniformity in Quality. We can with the utmost confidence recommend the qualities at

1/4, 1/6, 1/8, 2/=, and 2/4 per lb.,

And the fine Ceylon Tea at

1/10 per lb.,

To those who can appreciate and enjoy really fine Tea. **5 lb. parcels and upwards sent post free.**

R. & J. CHRISTIE,

8 Findlay Street, | **178 New City Road,**
Cowcaddens. | Corner of Gardner St.,

198 and 200 GALLOWGATE,

GLASGOW.

ADVERTISEMENTS.

J. & C. BUCHANAN,

Grocers and . . . Provision Merchants,

BUCHANAN STREET,
BALFRON.

Agents for Mazawattee Tea and Cocoa.

HOUSE COAL.

Best Qualities delivered to any part of the surrounding District at Moderate Prices.

TRUCK LOADS SENT TO ANY STATION.

D. S. BUCHANAN,
COAL AGENT,
BALFRON.

BUCHANAN'S POPULAR ILLUSTRATED GUIDE

TO

STRATHENDRICK, ABERFOYLE AND DISTRICT.

Published by J. & C. Buchanan, Balfron.

1902.

ADVERTISEMENTS.

CONTENTS.

	PAGE
BALFRON—	
From the Station,	17
The Clachan,	18
Kepculloch Moor and Park Quarry,	22
The Village,	24
History and Industries,	27
Walks,	28
Water and Light,	29
Other Attractions,	29
Towards the Field Bridge,	30
From Balfron to Fintry,	33
The Abduction of Jean Kay,	35
Gerchew Well, Holm Church, and Balgair,	36
Walks, Drives, and Places of Interest,	39

CONTENTS.

	PAGE
FINTRY,	40
How to Get to Fintry,	41
Pursuits,	42
Hills and Glens and Places of Interest,	45
KILLEARN—	
From Fintry to Killearn,	51
The Prince's View,	54
The Village,	57
Outdoor Attractions,	58
George Buchanan's Monument,	58
The Churches,	59
Other Places of Interest and Mansions,	63
Pot of Gartness,	65
DRYMEN—	
The Village,	67
Notable Personages,	70
Rambles around Drymen,	74
Buchanan,	79
From Drymen to Balmaha,	80
KILMARONOCK—	
From Caldarvan Station,	84
Ross Priory,	87
From Gartocharn to Drymen,	90
BUCHLYVIE,	92
Leaving Buchlyvie by the East,	96
Arnprior,	96
Leaving Buchlyvie by the West,	97
KIPPEN—	
Pursuits,	102
Some Interesting Features,	103
Natural Features and Prospects,	106
Places of Interest,	107

CONTENTS.

THE LAKE OF MENTEITH— PAGE
    From Port of Menteith Station to the Lake, 108
    The Port, 109
    The Lake, 110
    The Islands, 110
    Inchmahome, 110
    The Priory, 111
    Queen Mary's Residence, 112
    Angling, 113
    Walks and Prospects, 114

GARTMORE, 117

ABERFOYLE, 124
    The Clachan Inn, 125
    The Ancient Clachan, 126
    The Modern Clachan, 126
    Natural Features, 127
    The Coulter, 128
    "The Long Low Bridge," 128
    The Old Church and Churchyard, 128
    The Golf Course, 129
    The Churches, 130
    To Loch Ard, Loch Chon, and Stronachlachar, 130
    From Aberfoyle to the Trossachs, 135
    Popular Drives and Walks to Scenes of "The Lady of the Lake" and Romance of "Rob Roy," 137

FROM THE MOUNTAIN TOPS, 139

CYCLING IN AND ABOUT STRATHENDRICK, 143
    The Endrick, 147

ANGLING, 149

SOME GEOLOGICAL FEATURES OF STRATHENDRICK, 153

BOTANICAL NOTES, 156

FARMING IN STRATHENDRICK, 160

LIST OF ILLUSTRATIONS.

Map of District.
Contents Page—Old Trees and Parish Church, Balfron.

	FACING PAGE
BALFRON, LOOKING TO CAMPSIE FELLS,	17
CLACHAN OAK, BELL TREE, AND PARISH CHURCH, BALFRON,	20
BALFRON, LOOKING TO NORTH,	29
THE ENDRICK, "UP THE DAM," BALFRON,	32
FINTRY BRIDGE,	40
THE "LOUP" OF FINTRY,	48
KILLEARN, LOOKING TO CAMPSIE FELLS,	52
GEORGE BUCHANAN'S MONUMENT, KILLEARN,	56
CHURCHYARD AND OLD PARISH CHURCH, KILLEARN,	61
POT OF GARTNESS,	65
THE SQUARE, DRYMEN,	72
DRYMEN BRIDGE,	81
MAINS CASTLE, KILMARONOCK,	88
BUCHLYVIE,	96
KIPPEN,	105
PRIORY OF INCHMAHOME,	112
GARTMORE, FROM CROSS,	117
BAILIE NICOL JARVIE HOTEL, ABERFOYLE,	125
OLD ABERFOYLE,	129
TROSSACHS PIER,	137
BALMAHA PIER, LOCH LOMOND,	145
LOCH ARD,	160

PREFACE.

This opportunity is taken to thank all who have so kindly and willingly assisted in the preparation of this guide. Great care has been taken to prevent mistakes, but should any be found, the publishers will be pleased to be notified of such, and have them corrected in future editions.

D. S. B.

Balfron, May, 1902.

INTRODUCTION.

Strathendrick, Aberfoyle, and District.

THE beautiful valley of Strathendrick, in the west of Stirlingshire, watered by the stream from which it derives its name, is not nearly so well known as its attractions deserve. Within twenty miles of the great capital of the west, on the northern side of the Campsie Fells, this finely wooded and watered Strath lies in view of the Highland Bens. Yet to few is it well known, except to those who have been born and bred within it, and for whom it possesses a charm which even long absence and distant wanderings can never dispel. Bounded on the south by the Campsie range, and on the north by the breezy moorland, stretching away to the Perthshire mountains, Strathendrick extends in a south-westerly direction to Loch Lomond, where the Endrick discharges its waters. Narrow at the upper end, where it issues between Skiddhu (Blackwing) and the Meikle Bin, the valley broadens and extends, on either side of the river, till it becomes a fair region of wood, water, and rich pasture lands. The air is pure and bracing, and the scenery affords endless attractions to the lover of the picturesque.

Aberfoyle and district, adjoining Strathendrick, and occupying the south-west corner of Perthshire, has been immortalized by Sir Walter Scott in "The Lady of the Lake" and "Rob Roy." The scenic splendour of mountain, vale and lake, is unsurpassed, and over all rests a nameless fascination, "a something more exquisite still," created by the genius of Scott, which glorified everything it touched.

It is only within recent years that anything at all has been done to render the district more accessible or desirable as a holiday resort, and even yet there are few attractions besides those of Nature. But these are manifold, and no one with an out-door hobby need lack scope or encouragement.

Fishing in loch and river, glen and moorland burn, awaits the rod; trout, pike, and salmon in their season reward the angler.

The cyclist will find a new interest, possibly a new love for his pastime and its attendant pleasures in a district so eminently suited to him, while the photographing visitor need never be at a loss to find subjects upon which to practise his skill.

Golf, that indispensable adjunct of leisure, is encouraged in different parts by the provision of three good courses, a number which is likely to increase.

Those who are seeking a new place for a quiet, restful, and invigorating summer holiday, away from the sounds of factory or forge, and the engrossing fluctuations of the mart, would do well to turn their thoughts to the lovely valley of the Endrick, or the classic district of Aberfoyle. For the guidance of such this book is published.

LIST OF CHURCHES.

Place.	Denomination.	Minister.
Aberfoyle,	Established,	Rev. W. M. Taylor.
Do.,	St. Mary's Episcopal,	Rev. G. W. Paterson, M.A.
Balfron,	Established,	Rev. Alexander Slessor.
Do.,	United Free,	Rev. James Lindsay, M.A.
Do.,	Roman Catholic,	Rev. Canon Hannan.
Buchanan,	Established,	Rev. W. H. Macleod, B.D.
Buchlyvie,	Established,	Rev. John A. Macdonald.
Do.,	United Free,	Rev. G. W. S. Cowie.
Drymen,	Established,	Rev. John Roy, M.A.
Do.,	United Free,	Rev. Andrew Wilson, M.A.
Fintry,	Established,	Rev. Wm. L. Campbell, B.D.
Gartmore,	Established,	Rev. J. Christie Johnston.
Do.,	United Free,	Rev. Malcolm M'Lean.
Killearn,	Established,	Rev. A. Gordon Mitchell.
Do.,	United Free,	Rev. Hugh Sanderson.
Kilmaronock,	Established,	Rev. Wm. Boyd, M.A.
Do.,	United Free,	Rev. James Dunlop.
Kippen,	Established,	Rev. J. G. Dickson, M.A.
Do.,	United Free,	Rev. H. W. Hunter, M.A.
Port of Menteith,	Established,	Rev. Charles Edward Stuart.

In all the Presbyterian Churches the Sabbath service is held at 12 noon, and also occasionally in the evening.
St. Mary's Episcopal, Aberfoyle, meets at 11.30 a.m. and 6 p.m.
Roman Catholic, Balfron, every alternate Sabbath at 11.30 a.m.

BALFRON, LOOKING TO CAMPSIE FELLS.

Guide to Strathendrick.

Balfron.

THE most competent etymologists say that the word Balfron is derived from Bal-fruin (Celtic), the town of mourning, and this derivation is supported by (or supports) an old tradition as to the origin of the name. It relates that the inhabitants had gone to a distance to celebrate some religious rites, leaving their young people at home. On their return they found that some wolves from the surrounding forest had devoured many of their children, and hence Bal-fruin, the town of mourning.

From the Station.

The village of Balfron is two miles from the station. Conveyances meet all the Glasgow trains, and the drive is pleasant and exhilarating. Immediately on leaving the station a large stretch of country meets the view; hill and dale, field and wood, composing a picture of the greatest beauty and interest. Fully a mile from the station, on the left, is the entrance to *Camoquhill Douglas*, prettily situated by the side of a picturesque little glen. The lodge-gates on the right form the entrance to *Ballindalloch House*, the property of Mr Henry Cooper. The ancient and honourable family of Cunningham at one time held this estate. William, 9th Earl of Glencairn, and Lord Chancellor of Scotland, was once the chief heritor in Balfron. The next entrance to the right leads to the parish manse. From the top of the *Ibert Hill* there is one of the finest views in Strathendrick, both of the valley, and the rugged peaks of the Grampians. Ibert means sacrifice, and in fancy we can picture the ancient Druids celebrating their bloody rites in the recesses of the great forest which then covered the district. *Spittal*, the name of a farm a little to the north, is another instance of a single word testifying to past history. This brings us down to the heroic and stirring times of chivalry when the Templars were a power in the land. On the suppression of their order the lands belonging to them fell into the hands of the Knights Hospitallers, whose numerous possessions may still be traced by the prevalence of the place-name "Spittal."

The Clachan.

The visitor next enters the *Clachan*. This was the ancient village, which consisted only of a few picturesque houses, grouped round the village green, in the centre of which stood the Old Clachan Tree.

ADVERTISEMENTS.

M. DRUMMOND,

Grocer and Provision Merchant,

BALFRON.

PATENT AND OTHER MEDICINES
IN STOCK.

LICENSED TO SELL METHYLATED SPIRITS.

B. MOLLOY,

DRESS AND COSTUME MAKER,
BALFRON.

STYLE, FIT, AND COMFORT GUARANTEED.

Diploma for Cosmopolitan System of Dressmaking.
A Limited Number of Pupils received.

Balfron Emporium.

LARGE SELECTION OF FANCY GOODS.

Variety of "Present from" Goods in Glass and China.

BOOTS AND SHOES.

A. BEDDIE.

ADVERTISEMENTS.

Wm. Lockhart & Sons,

Bakers and Purveyors,

BUCHANAN STREET,

BALFRON.

BREAD and PASTRY made from Best Ingredients and Highest Grade Flours.

Montgomery's Patent "BERMALINE" Bread.

SEED CAKES,   LUNCH CAKES,
   MADEIRA CAKES,   SULTANA CAKES,
MARRIAGE, BIRTHDAY, AND CHRISTENING CAKES.

SCOTCH SHORTBREAD—
Plain, Fancy, and with Mottoes.

EXCURSION AND PIC-NIC PARTIES PURVEYED FOR.

VANS deliver Bi-Weekly in Gartmore, Buchlyvie, Fintry, and Killearn Districts.

ORDERS PROMPTLY ATTENDED TO.

Telegrams—"LOCKHART, BALFRON."

CLACHAN OAK, BELL TREE, AND CHURCH, BALFRON.

At the east end of the green, as now, stood the Parish Church, whilst the school was at the part where Orchardlands now is. There is a tradition that when the Covenanters fought and won the battle of Drumclog, the scholars planted a tree in commemoration of the event. This tree is probably the old ash on the borders of the churchyard, which would then be immediately in front of the schoolhouse. It was used in later years as a belfry, but probably not after the church and bell-spire were built in 1832. The position the bell occupied is, however, still conspicuous, and the apparent age of the tree corresponds with the date of the event.

The Clachan Oak stands at the entrance to the Clachan from the north. This venerable relic of primeval times, although in decay for the last 100 years, is still a "hale green tree," and has wrapped up within it a record of the history of the parish for many centuries. There is a tradition that Wallace rested his weary limbs under its shade. Beneath its spreading boughs a grim tragedy is said to have taken place about the end of the eighteenth century. Attached to the tree were the "jougs"—a kind (or an unkind) of iron collar, which was fastened round the necks of offenders in such public places as the Kirk Gate or at the Market Cross. The wife of a vagrant, accused of pilfering, was secured in the "jougs," and her husband sought to alleviate her miseries somewhat by sitting on the public green at her feet, but getting wearied of this durance vile, he stepped over to what is still known as the Clachan House to "light his pipe." Here he lingered for some considerable time, and returned to find his wife dead. She had got irritated evidently at his prolonged absence, and in her impatience, had kicked away the stones on which she stood, or they had slid in some way from beneath her, and so she was strangled in the "jougs!" The incident gave people such a shock that the punishment of the "jougs" in the parish was henceforward abandoned.

Near the old oak stands the *Parish Church*, erected in 1832 and remodelled in 1882 through the generosity of the present minister, Rev. Alexander Slessor. It is a neat and picturesque building, around whose ivied walls lie the quiet graves of many past generations.

In the possession of Mr. Alexander Fairlie Wilson, of Burnbrae, the descendant of a family of proprietors whose connection with the Clachan dates far back into the eighteenth century, and the best living authority on matters relating to this historical spot, there is an old broadsword which is a relic of a dark deed of blood. It was picked up at the Clachan after a fray in which one of the Buchanans of Cremannan was shot. Tradition credits the deed to Rob Roy's men, who were infuriated at Cunningham of Ballindalloch, who issued the warrant for the seizure of Rob's sons in connection with the abduction of Jean Kay of Edenbellie. The men were in waiting in the village ale-house, and seeing Cremannan pass by, they mistook him for Cunningham, and shot him dead.

Kepculloch Moor and Park Quarry.

The road going northward leads by Kepculloch Moor and Buchlyvie to Stirling. If a whiff of pure mountain air is wanted, the visitor will find it along this road, for this is where it is "made." Before proceeding far one of the most magnificent of panoramas bursts into view. Away in front are the beautiful hills of Perthshire and West Stirling, with Ben Ledi, Ben Voirlich, Ben Venue, Ben More, and Ben Lomond towering to the sky; while in the foreground may be seen the beautifully situated village of Gartmore, with Gartmore House nestling 'mid the trees, and the surrounding classic country of Menteith. And above all and around all the everlasting hills, the Grampians in front, Gargunnock Hills to the east, with a glimpse of the Ochils, the Campsie Fells south, and westward the Kilpatrick Hills and peaks about Loch Lomond.

A short distance from the first milestone, on the right, is an old cart track through the fields leading to a fine trap dyke known as the *Park Quarry*. This quarry was opened about 1813, and worked till lately as a quarry for road metal. It is one of those great fissures in the earth's crust, probably due to contraction or some such cause, and which has been filled up with other matter of volcanic origin. When cooling this matter contracted, leaving a narrow fissure between its sides and the adjoining sandstone, which it has baked very hard. This in turn has been filled up with a heavy white silicate in a fine crystalline form. This great dyke is on an average 15 feet broad, and has been worked for a distance of 234 yards. The quarry can also be reached from the middle of Kepculloch Moor by a cart track. The lower part is 200 yards from the gate.

The Village.

Leaving the Clachan by the road fringed by ancient oak trees, and leading to the south, the village is soon reached. At the entrance, on the left, is a memorial fountain erected to the memory of Dr. M'Candlish, a late popular physician. Buchanan Street begins at this point, and sloping southward, faces Dungoyne, the southern terminus from this point of the Campsie range. Minor streets branch off eastwards, and devious "back roads" form quiet retreats where the visitor may loiter.

In addition to the Parish Church at the Clachan, the other buildings of importance are the United Free Church (1882), an R.C. Chapel, a new district police station, the British Linen Co. Bank, and the requisite complement of shops, hotels, etc. The United Free Church was built from a fund, £1000 of which was contributed by the late Mr. Michael Robertson, banker. Mr. Robertson was a man of rare natural gifts, his witticisms resembling intermittent flashes of sheet lightning, illuminating every object but hurting no one. When he died it was said of him—

"But never in the days that are to be,
 The same old type of true man will be found,
Till winding stream roll upward from the sea,
 And pine-clad mountain sink into the ground!

He was as courteous as the knights of old,
 And softly gave the stroke that needs must fall;
His wit was keen, but it was never cold,
 And a rich humour sparkled in it all."

ADVERTISEMENTS.

JAMES CLEMENT,

Grocer, - -

Provision &

Grain - - -

Merchant, -

BUCHANAN STREET, BALFRON.

HOME-CURED BACON—A Speciality.

COUNTRY EGGS DAILY.

ORDERS CALLED FOR AND DELIVERED.

Branch Shop—212 Dumbarton Road, PARTICK.

ADVERTISEMENTS.

Ballindalloch Hotel,
BALFRON.

FIRST-CLASS . . .
TOURISTS' AND COMMERCIAL HOTEL.

GOOD CENTRE FROM WHICH TO VISIT
Loch Lomond, Lake of Menteith,
Aberfoyle and Trossachs.

EXHILARATING AIR.
SCENERY IN IMMEDIATE NEIGHBOURHOOD
OF SURPASSING BEAUTY.

Special arrangements for Boarding Week-End,
Week, Month, or longer period.

C.T.C. HEADQUARTERS.

LUNCHEONS.   DINNERS.   TEAS.

The ENDRICK, a famous Trout stream, 3 minutes' walk.

POSTING IN ALL ITS BRANCHES.

WM. HOSIE, Proprietor.

Telegrams: "Hosie, Balfron."

History and Industries.

Up till the end of the eighteenth century Balfron was chiefly, if not wholly, an agricultural parish. Mr. Robert Dunmore of Ballikinrain, a public-spirited gentleman, established an agency for the manufacture of calicoes, but this proving unprofitable, he joined with others in the introduction of cotton spinning, a large mill being built in 1789. This industry was sucessfully carried on by Messrs J. & A. Buchanan of Carston, who probably gave the name "Buchanan" to the main street; by Messrs J. Finlay & Co., Glasgow, a firm still in existence, who bought it from the Buchanans in 1793; by the Jeffries, and latterly by Messrs H. W. Pollock & Co., who set up in it a shirt manufactory. This firm gave up business in October, 1893, and in 1898 the building was purchased by Mr. Archibald E. Orr-Ewing, of Ballikinrain, and demolished.

It was the introduction of cotton spinning that originated and supported the present village. To provide the necessary accommodation for the employees and their families, a neat and regular village was built, containing 105 new houses, "with 430 rooms in which were fire places," as is the quaint description given in a record of the time. Hand-loom weaving long flourished in the village, there being at one time between 300 and 400 looms working. Then, as the old folks tell, the cheery sound of the shuttle could be heard in almost every house, and the weavers, who read and thought much over their looms, were a race of strong, intelligent men, who took no small interest in the political and social movements of the times. Now the last shuttle is silent.

The population of the parish at the last census was 1092, compared with 2057 in 1831, while the population of the village in 1901 was 737, compared with 885 in 1891. Apart from a small branch shirt factory, employing about 40 young women, the inhabitants for the most part depend upon agricultural and other outdoor labour.

Few villages are so pleasantly situated, and fewer have so lovely a series of prospects. There is ground for the remark which one of her worthy sons made to a gentleman on his return from a tour round the world. The traveller was viewing with satisfaction his own countryside, and happening to say, "I have been round the world, and yet I have never seen any place equal to L——." "Ah!" was the quick rejoinder, "you have never seen Balfron."

Walks.

One of the principal attractions of a holiday resort are its walks and its opportunities for getting off the beaten track—the hard high road. Of these Balfron can boast of not a few. In fact there are not many country villages where one's choice is so rich, varied, and unrestrained. The finer beauties of the land are only to be found in such quiet nooks and lonely places that patience, time, and familiarity are required to discover and fully appreciate them. Endless enjoyment may be found in wandering by the lovely banks of the Endrick, or angling in its

BALFRON, LOOKING TO NORTH.   *Photo. by M. A. Robertson, Alloa.*

limpid waters, tempting the tempting, wiling the wily trout, following those pleasant paths that lead by fragrant hedgerows and into romantic glens; or keeping by the high road (on foot or wheel), to view from one or other of these points of vantage, easily accessible, the grand array of northern mountains and silver expanse of the Queen of Scottish Lakes; or climbing the hills, where the whole beautiful Strath and wide expanse beyond may be seen spread out like a huge map at one's feet.

Water and Light.

The village has a supply of gravitation water of excellent quality from Spittal Well. There is also a connection with the Glasgow Corporation water, which can be drawn upon in the event of scarcity. The streets are lit with lamps. This village, it may be noted, was one of the first to enjoy the use of coal gas, introduced by and abolished with the cotton spinning industry.

Other Attractions.

Balfron is a good centre in which to spend a holiday. The natives are hospitable and kind, accommodation can be had at moderate rates, children have ample scope, the banks of the Endrick forming a never failing attraction, while the cyclist has an endless variety of roads leading to places of interest at an easy distance.

In recent years a great source of attraction have

been the cheap circular drives. Perhaps in no part of Scotland are drives, through such interesting and varied scenery, to be got at such cheap rates.

Towards the Field Bridge.

Leaving the village by the south, Elcho House is seen on the right. This, once the residence of Mr. Andrew Jeffrey, one of the proprietors of the cotton mill, was subsequently owned and tenanted by Mr. John M. Dawson, and afterwards by the late Mr. Richard Barnwell, managing director of the Fairfield Shipbuilding Co., Ltd., and is still the residence of Mr. Barnwell's family.

On the left, at this point an avenue leads to the site of the Old Mill, already referred to, and the walk, *par excellence*, of the district—"Up the Dam." A native thus apostrophized the ruins of the Old Mill—

>Could no hand arrest decline,
>   Or place once more upon thy brow
>The fallen crown which once was thine,
>   Ere thou adversity did'st know?
>Alas, for man and all his deeds!
>   When they have served the passing hours,
>And satisfied life's urgent needs,
>   Are cast aside like scentless flowers.
>
>Within thy gates, the weedy sod
>   Has taken deep abiding root
>Upon the pathway that was trod
>   By blithesome village maiden's foot.
>The whirring wheels no more resound,
>   No more the laugh, the jest, the song—
>And only Echo can be found
>   To give the lips of Death a tongue.

ADVERTISEMENTS.

JAMES HAMILTON

(Successor to ANDREW GRAHAM),

Carrier and Contractor,

 BALFRON.

GLASGOW QUARTERS—QUEEN ST. GOODS STATION.
TUESDAYS AND FRIDAYS.

BALFRON QUARTERS—DUNMORE STREET.
MONDAYS AND THURSDAYS.

PARCELS to or from GLASGOW promptly delivered.
CARTING IN ALL ITS BRANCHES.

JAMES HAMILTON,

Grocer and Grain Merchant,

DUNMORE STREET,

 BALFRON.

Large Stock of FEEDING STUFFS
always on hand.

☞ Orders for Articles not in Stock got on the Shortest Notice.

ADVERTISEMENTS.

"The Macgregor" Posting Establishment,
BALFRON.

Telegrams: "CLEMENT, BALFRON."   JAMES CLEMENT, *Proprietor.*

Proprietor of the "North British Railway 'Bus."

THROUGH TICKETS are issued by the Railway Company from Queen Street, Glasgow, direct to Balfron Village with "The Macgregor" Coaches only.

DRIVES ARRANGED FOR EXCURSION PARTIES.
SPECIAL TERMS ON APPLICATION.

Char-a-Banc, Brakes, Covered Omnibuses, Waggonettes, Dog Carts, Landau, Brougham, etc.

Special Carriages sent to Station to meet Parties on receipt of Telegram or Letter.

THE ENDRICK, "UP THE DAM," BALFRON.

Proceeding along the road which leads to Glasgow (19 miles), via Killearn (2 miles), the Printers' Row, with a fine southern exposure, and in front a delightful picture of hill, dale, and water, is passed, and the Ballindalloch, or, as Balfron people invariably call it, the "Field" Bridge, half-a-mile distant, is reached. This bridge spans the Endrick; and connects the parishes of Balfron and Killearn, and takes its title, as does the Printers' Row, from the old time printfield which flourished near by.

From Balfron to Fintry.

Leaving the village by Dunmore Street, so named after the founder of the village, a few hundred yards along on the left is the *United Free Church Manse*, built to designs furnished by Alexander Thomson, the famous architect. "Greek Thomson," as he was known in his profession, on account of his preference for the Grecian style of architecture, was a native of Balfron, being born in Printers' Row, in the low situated house opposite Neilson Terrace, at the lower extremity of the village. Fine specimens of his genius may be seen in some of the public buildings in Glasgow. He is seen at his best in the Egyptian Halls, Union Street, Queen's Park United Free Church, the front of which has been described as an extraordinary concentration of art; and St. Vincent Street and Caledonia Road United Free Churches.

At the corner of Kilfasset Farm, at the junction of Dunmore Street and the road leading to Balgair, is a beautifully defined circular mound, locally known as the "*Round Wood*" or "*Roman Camp.*" It is surrounded by a trench, which, at the south-east corner, leads into Neil's Burn. The surface on the top is flat, and measures 40 paces in diameter, while at the base the circumference is 190 paces. It is overgrown with oak and birch trees. On the opposite side of the road in the moor are some half-a-dozen parallel trenches in fairly good preservation, and the land here, on the northern side, gives no evidence of having been under cultivation. The commanding situation of the mound, its construction, and the adjacent trenches, leave no doubt as to its military origin, but the period to which it belongs is still an unsolved mystery.

At the foot of the brae before reaching Woodend Farm is the entrance to *Neil's Glen*, or better known locally as the "*White Yett*" *Glen*.

> There the gowden sun comes keekin' through the leaves abune sae green,
> An' wi' his rays enchantin' lichtens up the fairy scene;
> Ither places may be bonnie, but the bonniest I ken,
> An' the spot lo'ed best o' ony is the White Yett Glen.

This glen is a favourite walk and a pleasant one, returning to the village by what is known as "the dam." A seat at the side of the burn, formed out of rock, is called the *Lovers' Seat*.

From a little beyond Woodend the scenery is most varied and beautiful. Up the slope towards the Campsie Fells is Ballikinrain Castle, a fine new mansion built by the late Sir Archibald Orr-Ewing, Bart., M.P., with beautiful pine woods growing around. Not less beautiful, though less conspicuously situated, the old mansion stands close to the river amid fine old trees.

Passing the ancient wood of *Kiltrochan* on the right, and taking the first road to the left, at Dalfoil Farm, about ¾ of a mile distant, is *Edenbellie*, where, prominent on a hill, stands the *Old Holm Secession Church*, one of the first Secession churches to be founded. It has been converted into a cattle shed. Crowds from far and near waited upon the ministry of men who laboured in connection with this church, and whose memory is still fragrant. One of them was Dr. James Thomson, granduncle of the late Mr. Comrie Thomson, the famous advocate. At this spot stood one of the mansion-houses of the renowned Napiers of Merchiston, which has been claimed as the birth-place of the most celebrated of that family, John Napier (1550-1617), the inventor of logarithms.

The Abduction of Jean Kay.

There lived at Edenbellie a young and comely heiress called Jean Kay or Wright. She married young, but in about a year was left a widow. No less a personage than Rob Oig, the youngest son of Rob Roy, desired to marry her. His suit was rejected, but the gallant was determined, so leaving Balquhidder with three brothers and five other men, he proceeded to Edenbellie and carried off the reluctant lady by force. The little company is said to have proceeded to Rowardennan, where a sham marriage ceremony was gone through, but the romantic lover paid dear for his exploit, as three years after he was hanged for it at Edinburgh. Jean Kay died in Glasgow on 4th October, 1751. It is worthy of note that the present occupier of the house, which adjoined the two-storeyed house in which Jean Kay lived, is a descendant of Thomas Neilson, the principal witness in the case against young Rob, and the eighth in the direct line who has resided here.

Gerchew Well, Holm Church, and Balgair.

A little beyond Dailfoil there is a road to the right, down which, about 200 yards, there is a stile over the fence, only a few feet from the famous *Gerchew Well*, on the banks of the Endrick. Here the visitor can repose for a time under the shade of the trees, and quench his thirst in its pure, cool, and bubbling waters. The road across the Endrick at Greystone, 2 miles from the village, is the more direct, but we will take the longer road via Balgair to Fintry. At this point, standing on a charming site on the banks of the Endrick, are the *United Free Church and Manse of the Holm of Balfron*. This congregation is now united with Balfron Church under the ministry of the Rev. James Lindsay, M.A. The Rev. Ebenezer Erskine, one of the founders of the Secession Church, preached to large audiences on the burnside just below, and on one occasion is said to have baptised as many as thirty children. By the

ADVERTISEMENTS.

ROBERT TAIT,

FAMILY BUTCHER,

BUCHANAN STREET, BALFRON.

Always on hand a regular supply of PRIME BEEF and MUTTON, also LAMB and VEAL in their Season.

CORNED BEEF AND PICKLED TONGUES.

ORDERS CALLED FOR AND PUNCTUALLY ATTENDED TO.

VAN CALLS AS FOLLOWS—
- MONDAY—BALLIKINRAIN, FINTRY, and HILL OF BALGAIR.
- TUESDAY—BUCHLYVIE and BALLAT DISTRICT.
- FRIDAY—BALLIKINRAIN, FINTRY, and BALGAIR.
- SATURDAY—BUCHLYVIE and BALLAT DISTRICT.

Morning Evening and Weekly **Newspapers.**

Periodicals and Magazines.

PAPERS DELIVERED MORNING AND EVENING.

Bibles and Hymnaries.

LARGE SELECTION OF . . .

Local View Goods.

Visitors will find these goods suitable mementoes, and well adapted for Presents.

BUCHANAN, BALFRON.

☞ List kept of Houses and Apartments to Let.

side of this burn, in the Holm Glen, is *St. Kessog's Well*, near to which tradition says St. Kessog, patron saint of the Earl of Lennox, is buried.

A mile further east is the *Hill of Balgair*, from which the view down into the hollow around Fintry is, on a summer evening, of surpassing beauty. The stranger should not miss a chat with some of the kindly and well-informed inhabitants of Balgair, and a visit to the old, unfinished, and yet ruinous mansion. of this name is pathetically interesting. From "the Hill" a winding and romantic road brings the traveller to Lernock, once a toll house, where the road runs southward to Fintry, and north and east to Kippen and beyond. A beautifully rural track (the old road to Stirling) strikes straight onwards along the foot of the Gargunnock Hills. The ascent of Skiddhu near here will meet with ample reward, as it commands a wide prospect east and west. At Lernock are the ruins of an old schoolhouse, where past generations were well taught spelling and the Catechism.

Between Lernock and Fintry lies the farm of *Provanston*, the birth-place of the late Dr. John Edmond of London, in 1816. Dr. Edmond was a preacher of great power. As a preacher to the young he had few equals. Several interesting works were published by him, chief of which are "Scripture Stories in Verse," "Children's Charter," and the "Children's Church in the House." The latter work has attained a wide and merited popularity. He died 6th October, 1893.

Walks, Drives, and Places of Interest.

Name.	Distance from Balfron Village.
"Up the Dam,"	Foot of Village.
The Camp or "Round" Wood,	½ mile.
Edenbellie,	1¾ miles.
Gerchew Well,	1½ miles.
Loup of Fintry,	7 miles.
Sir John de Graham's Castle,	8½ miles.
Macher Glen,	1½ miles.
Killearn,	2 miles.
Pot of Gartness,	3 miles.
Finnich Glen,	4½ miles.
Balmaha (Loch Lomond),	9 miles.
Kepculloch Moor and Park Quarry,	1½ miles
Lake of Menteith,	12 miles.
Aberfoyle,	9 miles.
Loch Ard,	12 miles.
Trossachs,	18 miles.

Fintry.

FINTRY derives its name from having been inhabited by the early race of Fingalian heroes, from *Fean*, a giant, and *tre*, a country, namely the country of the giants.

In a place like Fintry, "remote, unfriended, solitary, slow," one does not look for much change even in a few hundred years, yet cannot fail to be struck with the unusual adherence to old tradition as manifested to this day in the very large proportion of handsome, stalwart men.

There are three hamlets or villages in the parish, Newtown or the modern village, the Clachan or ancient village, three-quarters of a mile further east, and containing the church, built in 1823; and fully a quarter of a mile further east still, the Gonachan, near the bridge which here crosses the Endrick.

When Mr. Peter Spiers, of Culcreuch, built a cotton factory in 1794, he was under the necessity of providing accommodation for the many hands employed. That was the genesis of Newtown, the present village. The village is charmingly situated on rising ground on the banks of the Endrick, which has its source in the north hills almost immediately behind Fintry in Gargunnock parish. The houses are for

FINTRY BRIDGE.

the most part on one side of the road, and on the opposite side gardens slope down to the river's brink. Lying at the base of the hills, Fintry reminds one of an Alpine village. The sun scarcely strikes it in winter, but in summer it forms an ideal retreat, in the centre of a quiet pastoral region, far from the din of cities and the disturbing whistle of the locomotive. Its position is central, being about 8 miles from eight railway stations, viz., Lennoxtown, Campsie Glen, Dungoyne, Killearn, Gartness, Balfron, Buchlyvie, and Kippen.

How to Get to Fintry.

From Glasgow Fintry is best reached by taking rail to Lennoxtown, and then walking or driving over the Craw Road, a distance of $8\frac{1}{4}$ miles. "Craw" Road has been defined "as the crow flies," or "the Caur or Car Road." If the weather be fine, to walk is preferable. For almost 3 miles the road is uphill, but the bracing air, magnificent scenery, and pleasant resting-places on the soft turf by the way, combine to make one forget all fatigue. Human habitations for a time are out of sight, and not even a shrub or a tree is to be seen. The Muir Toll, or Half-Way House, is at length reached. This house is a welcome sight to the weary traveller on a stormy night, and even a relief in the bright noon of a summer's day. Above Lurg Farm the road takes a sharp turn, and a glorious prospect bursts into view. The stretch of country lying in front from Port of Menteith round by Aberfoyle, with the majestic Ben Lomond and numerous peaks of the Highland hills, is magnificent. In a few minutes the Clachan of Fintry is descried, with the village in the distance. Either is soon reached, and a "tousie" tea can then be discussed with comfort and the utmost relish. It only requires a very short residence among the good folks of Fintry to confirm what has been said about the roads. It is alleged that the roads into Fintry are better known than the roads out, because the people are so hospitably inclined that it is with great reluctance people ever leave it.

Pursuits.

Apart from agricultural and pastoral pursuits there are no industries in the parish of Fintry. The grazing of sheep and cattle principally engages the attention of the farmer. In 1841 a cotton mill was in full operation, employing 260 hands, and at the same time a distillery, which annually produced 70,000 gallons of whisky. This whisky is said to have been of excellent quality, no doubt owing to the peculiar virtues of the water from Spinner's Well. The sceptical visitor may sample the water "still." The ruins of a paper mill are yet to be seen on the south-east of Culcreuch Avenue.

The population of the parish in 1831 was 1051, and 314 in 1901, the great decrease being accounted for by the ejectment of smaller tenants owing to the enlargement of the farms, and to a greater extent by the collapse of the cotton industry.

ADVERTISEMENTS.

FINTRY INN.

TOURISTS and VISITORS

Will find this a comfortable and homely place at which to take

Luncheon or Tea.

Larger Parties are catered for on receiving due Notice.

JOHN FERGUSON,
Proprietor.

Telegrams—"FERGUSON, FINTRY."

ADVERTISEMENTS.

WM. EDMOND,

Grain, Provision, and General Merchant,

FINTRY.

LARGE AND SELECT STOCK OF . . .
GROCERIES, PROVISIONS, AND FEEDING STUFFS,
DELF, CHINA, AND GLASS,
IRONMONGERY, HOSIERY, BOOTS AND SHOES.

VAN delivers Goods as follows:—
TUESDAY—BALGAIR, GREYSTONE, and BALLIKINRAIN.
THURSDAY—DENNY ROAD as far as CARNOCK.

ALL WANTS ARE PROMPTLY ATTENDED TO.

WM. EDMOND,

Carriage Hirer, Carrier, & Contractor,

FINTRY.

During July and August a Conveyance meets specified Trains at LENNOXTOWN on MONDAYS, WEDNESDAYS, and SATURDAYS.

On receipt of Letter or Telegram a Conveyance will await any Train.

LUGGAGE and PARCELS conveyed as directed.

Agent for HOUSE COAL.

Telegrams—"EDMOND, FINTRY."

Hills and Glens and Places of Interest.

The interesting features of Fintry are its hills and glens. Beginning with the hills on the south of Fintry and passing from west to east, the first feature of note is the *Corrie of Balglass*, in the parish of Killearn. This is a deep hollow in the form of a semicircle or caldron-shaped recess, running into the heart of the hill, where the rock rises precipitously to a height of some 600 or 700 feet. The strata in the rock are so distinctly marked as to suggest the idea of the tides dashing against it. Professor A. Geikie says it is a mistake to suppose that recesses of this kind have been caused by volcanic disturbance. *Dunmore* (1280 feet) is at the west end of the village. Visitors who like a good stiff bracing walk should make the ascent of this hill. Start in the morning, and with a good pair of legs and sound lungs the summit should be reached in forty minutes. The view from the top of the cairn is extensive. Loch Lomond is seen in the distance like a huge mirror, the Ben towering above in his majesty, and the nearer Strath below in all its beauty and variety of contour and colour.

Immediately below, in a spot called the *Covenanters' Hole*, was held one of the most memorable conventicles in Strathendrick. This "Hole" on the north shoulder of Dunmore, originally a deep depression with rock rising up sheer behind, is now filled up with fallen rock, but is still quite visible. The meeting took place on 18th May, 1679, fifteen days after the murder of Archbishop Sharp on Magus Muir, and among other prominent Covenanters present was John Balfour of Burley (or Burleigh), who, concerned in the death of the Archbishop, was flying from Fife to find an asylum among the Covenanters of the west. The sermon had scarcely begun when the meeting was disturbed by the arrival of a large party of foot and horse soldiers from Stirling. A skirmish took place, in which there was a good deal of firing, but little injury to either side. The military retired with only one prisoner, a herd laddie, whom for very shame they soon set free. The rock is still pointed out under which it is said the preacher's cloak was concealed.

The Spinners' Well must not be passed if the visitor wishes a cooling draught of real "mountain dew." It is about 300 yards to the north of the Covenanters' Hole, lower down the slope of the hill.

Cavalry Green, with the remains of a military encampment, north-east of Dunmore, dates probably from the time of the Covenanters. Here the Fintry Yeomanry, who were never called out, practised in peace the deadly sport of war.

Turf Hill, a little east of Dunmore, is also 1280 feet.

Dunine Glen, a beautifully wooded glen on the east side of Dunmore, the burn in which forms the boundary between Fintry and Killearn.

Dechrode, 1305 feet, noted for a cave, difficult of access, half-way up the rock, and said to lead to Dunmore, about half-a-mile to the west.

Dumbroch, 1664 feet, in shape, as seen from the road, like a whale's back.

Dumgoyle, 1395 feet, a rugged mass rising up from the Gonachan Glen, a glen of marvellous beauty, on the banks of which the hazel nut grows in great profusion.

The Meikle Bin, 1870 feet, the most prominent height in the Campsie Hills, a little to the south of the Craw Road, somewhat conical in appearance, and most easily ascended from the western side. Its summit commands one of the most extensive and beautiful views in the country, embracing as it does a striking view of the Grampian Range, the Abbey Craig, and the Ochils from Demyat to Glendevon, with the various towns along their base.

The Little Bin, 1446 feet, north-east of the Meikle Bin.

Moses' Glen, nearly opposite Woodfoot Cottage, and remarkable only for its name. In the heart of the Gargunnock Hills in Balfron parish, above the farm of Easter Glinns, is a wide gully, once notorious as the haunt of smugglers.

The North or Gargunnock Hills are a long, almost unbroken range of fine hills with but few peaks. Beginning again at the west we have

Stronend, at the angle of the Gargunnock Hills, facing south-west, and consisting of a double precipice, which, with its black serrated rock, has a grand appearance from the public road near Newtown.

The Dune, south-east from Stronend, a little conical hill, rising from the slope of the Gargunnock Hills, and just above Craigton, noted for its curious formation of basaltic pillars.

Gowk Stanes, of similar construction to above, are

a little further east, while immediately to the north of the Gowk Stanes is the *Reservoir*, which formerly provided power for the mills. It is now well stocked with magnificent Loch Leven trout, and the disciple of Izaak Walton may there, under permission, wile away many a happy hour and sundry unfortunate trout. At the foot of the hill, beneath Stronend, is the famous *Coal Pit Glen*, so called because of a disused coal pit in the neighbourhood. The distance from a railway station was perhaps too great for successful mining in Fintry.

The Wee Loup, or *Lover's Leap*, a beautiful little glen east on the Denny Road above Woodfoot Cottage. The title, Lover's Leap, has been given to this glen as it seems just such a place as that in which a disconsolate lover would seek to drown his unrequited love and himself probably.

The "Loup of Fintry."—About $2\frac{1}{2}$ miles to the east of the church on the Denny Road, the Endrick pours its waters over a precipitous rock 94 feet high. This is known as the "Loup of Fintry." When the river is in flood the fall presents a magnificent appearance. In its normal condition there are three breaks in the fall, but in flood time the water dashes over the rock, upwards of 30 yards wide, in one unbroken cataract, and rages with unbridled fury against the enormous masses of detached rock below.

A mile and a half east of the "Loup of Fintry," on the left of the Denny Road, in St. Ninians parish, are the ruins of *Sir John de Graham's Castle*. Burned by the English 600 years ago, this building has long been in ruins, and all that remain now are

THE "LOUP" OF FINTRY.

Photo. by M. A. Robertson, Alloa.

some stone ramparts and mounds of earth. Near the Castle stood a chapel with a burial-place, called the *Kirk of Muir*, where an annual open-air preaching or conventicle is still held and largely attended. Sir John de Graham (belonging to the same family as the Duke of Montrose), the faithful companion of Sir William Wallace, was born and lived here. He joined the patriot in his heroic endeavours to achieve the independence of his native country, and was slain while gallantly fighting at the battle of Falkirk, July 22nd, 1298. Wallace's lament over his dead body in the Metrical Chronicle of Blind Harry, is one of the most elegant passages in that romantic and popular narrative of the Scottish hero's exploits. The Minstrel represents him as saying—

> "My dearest brother that I ever had;
> My only friend when I was hard bestead;
> My hope, my health! Oh man of honour great,
> My faithful aid and strength in every strait,
> Thy matchless wisdom cannot here be told,
> Thy noble manhood, truth and courage bold,
> Wisely thou knew to rule and govern,
> Yes, virtue was thy chief and great concern,
> A bounteous hand, a heart as true as steel,
> A steady mind, most courteous, and genteel."

Culcreuch.—This mansion, which belongs to Mr. Walter Menzies, stands above the village. At one time it was owned by the Galbraiths, a powerful family in Strathendrick, later by the Napiers, and was subsequently bought by Mr. Peter Speirs, of the family of the Speirs of Elderslie, a gentleman whose memory will long be affectionately cherished for the great and practical interest he took in the affairs of the parish.

Craigton, belonging to Mr. Wm. Gibb, is situated about a mile east of Culcreuch, and above the Gonachan. Mr. Dun, the first laird, entered the *Glasgow Herald* Office as a boy, and afterwards became one of the proprietors. The Duns occupied the Lurg Farm near by for generations.

Sir Daniel Macnee, the distinguished artist, and one time President of the Royal Scottish Academy, was born in Fintry in 1806.

Killearn.

From Fintry to Killearn.

THE distance from Fintry to the village of Killearn is 7 miles. Leaving Fintry by the west, and proceeding in a north-westerly direction for 2 miles, a road on the left leads to the site of *Balglass Castle*, where within the old walls a farmhouse and offices have been built. Over a hundred years ago the old building was standing, and is said to have been "a large house or castle of an antiquated construction." When flying from his enemies this house once afforded a refuge to Sir William Wallace.

For some miles extends the beautiful estate of *Ballikinrain*, the property of Mr. Archibald E. Orr-Ewing. This estate for eighteen generations belonged to the Napier family, and was purchased by the late Sir Archibald Orr-Ewing, Bart., M.P., in 1861. Sir Archibald erected the splendid mansion on the higher grounds, and he also formed the fine gardens, and by his energy and enterprise the barren hillside was transformed into thriving plantations and cultivated fields. It was an exiled Ballikinrain youth who sang—

> I sometimes close my eyes and see
> Fair Endrick's placid stream,
> And muse on days that used to be,
> But now seem like a dream.
> Yet even in these other days,
> Fond memories linger still:
> The dear old house, the glen, the braes,
> The Castle on the hill.

The old mansion of Ballikinrain, occupied so long by the Napiers, is situated on the right near the river Endrick.

The next estate passed is *Boquhan*, owned by Mr. David Bryce-Buchanan. Following the march dyke between Ballikinrain and Boquhan, the *Earl's Seat* (1894 feet) is reached. This is the highest point of the Campsie Fells, and the parishes of Strathblane, Campsie, Fintry, and Killearn meet here. Opposite Branshogle Mill, on the left, is the entrance to the *Machar Glen*, a happy hunting-ground for lovers of ferns and a haunt of the geologist. About half-a-mile up the glen, on the right, is a cavity in the rock called *Rob Roy's Hole*, where the outlaw was in the habit of concealing himself when too closely pursued by his enemies. Half-a-mile further up to the east of the glen are to be seen the ruins of *Machar House*, where Rob Roy used to spend weeks at a time with his friend, Walter Buchanan, the laird of Machar.

A native, now residing in Canada, who spent child-

KILLEARN, LOOKING TO CAMPSIE FELLS.

hood's days in a farm near by, revisiting this scene in the Autumn of 1901, wrote—

> "Here, when we were bairns thegither,
> Mony a prank we used tae play,
> Rinnin' wild, we chased each ither,
> Helter-skelter doon the brae,
> Ower the glen, or 'mang the heather,
> Paidlin' in the Machar Burn,
> Guddlin' troots, or flo'ers did gether,
> Weel we kent its every turn."

Boquhan House, on the right of the Fintry Road, stands amidst noble beeches that have weathered many a storm. Within the memory of the present laird a large meal girnel occupied a corner in an outhouse which was used by Rob Roy for collecting the meal from the local lairds in return for his services in protecting their property.

A little further west, on the right, is *Parkhall House*, a substantial redstone mansion, recently built by Lady Connal. The site is only a few yards from the old mansion occupied so long by Sir Michael Connal, a well-known Glasgow citizen. Sir Michael possessed a unique personality, and took a great interest in educational and philanthropic agencies. He was a member of the Glasgow School Board from 1873 till his death in 1893, and during most of these years acted as chairman.

One of the finest views of the village of Balfron is to be had from this point, as it stands on the face of the hill, beautifully adorned by the foliage of its numerous trees. Immediately below is the hamlet of

Little Boquhan, half-way between the villages of Balfron and Killearn.

At the cross roads the road to the right leads to Balfron through Little Boquhan, that in front to Balfron Station, past Ballochruin Bridge, and that to the left to Killearn, a distance of ¾ of a mile. The hill here is called the Black Hill, and the pipes of the Glasgow Corporation Waterworks pass below the road.

Carbeth House is situated on the right near the banks of the Endrick. From 1482 till 1873 this house belonged to an influential branch of the family of Buchanan of that ilk. It is now the residence and property of Mr. David Wilson, a gentleman well-known as an authority in the department of Agricultural science.

The Prince's View.

From the milestone a little beyond Townhead, the finest prospect in Strathendrick is unfolded. "A rest for the weary" has been considerately placed here by Mr. Robert Buchanan, a worthy son of Killearn, and as Pat would put it, "is moighty convanient," not only for garrulous age and whispering lovers, but for weary pedestrians of every sort and condition. Seated here facing the west, one may look upon everything which can be desired in the ideal landscape. Away in front is Loch Lomond, "the Queen of Scottish Lakes," with its islands softened and melted and mingled in the distance, a beautiful panorama of woodland, richly cultivated fields, sunny slopes, swelling and undulating upwards to the heath-clad moors, they in turn

ADVERTISEMENTS.

W. G. MORRISON,
GROCER, GRAIN, AND PROVISION MERCHANT,
KILLEARN.

Provisions a Speciality.

SMOKED HAMS,
BUTTER AND CHEESE.
BACON, OWN CURING.
TEAS AND COFFEES, BLENDED AND PURE.
SPECIAL VALUE IN TEA, 2/ PER LB.

Large Stock of FEEDING STUFFS
Always on Hand.

Goods delivered by messenger in village, and by vans in surrounding district.

ADVERTISEMENTS.

DAVID FAIRLIE,

FAMILY BUCTHER,

KILLEARN.

PRIME BEEF and WEDDER MUTTON
Selected from the Best Home-Fed.

VANS deliver regularly in surrounding VILLAGES and DISTRICT.

POSTING ESTABLISHMENT.

OPEN AND CLOSE CARRIAGES ON HIRE.

CONVEYANCES AWAIT TRAIN ON RECEIPT OF LETTER OR TELEGRAM.

Drives to Surrounding Places of Interest arranged.

DAVID FAIRLIE,
KILLEARN,

Telegrams: "Fairlie, Killearn,"   *Proprietor.*

GEORGE BUCHANAN'S MONUMENT, KILLEARN.

meeting with and melting into what has been happily described as "Scotland's northern battlement of hills." His Majesty King Edward VII., then Prince of Wales, while visiting the district in September, 1899, was so enamoured of the grandeur of the scene that he desired to be driven over this part of the road twice. The view from this point is now known as the *Prince's View*.

The Village.

The village of Killearn is reached. It has a population of 318, while the population of the parish is 929. Killearn is said to be made up of three Celtic words, Kill-ear-rhin, meaning the cell or church of west point. The situation, at the western extremity of the Campsie Fells, confirms this etymology. The village, about a mile from the station, and $16\frac{1}{2}$ miles from Glasgow by road, is built on rising ground, commanding an extensive prospect. At first sight it appears plain, irregularly built, quiet and dull, but a closer acquaintance reveals one of the sweetest and neatest of villages. There is little wonder that it is so popular among the well-to-do class as a summer resort. The village itself has an aspect of peace, repose, and rural simplicity, while the neighbourhood is most pleasing and picturesque, the surrounding hills supplying a never-failing source of attraction. The natives of Killearn are a *bien* and thrifty people, some think a trifle exclusive, attached to the village and parish, and possessing in a marked degree the old Scottish characteristic of independence, practically exhibited in the fact that up till a comparatively recent date, the authorities did not find it necessary to adopt the legal method of assessment for the maintenance of the poor, the church-door collections, and later a voluntary assessment on the part of the heritors, being found sufficient for that purpose.

Water and Light.—Through the liberality of the late Mr. Alexander Buchanan of Messrs John Buchanan Bros., confectioners, Glasgow, and a native of Killearn, the village has an abundant supply of excellent gravitation water, and is also lit with lamps.

Outdoor Attractions.

A *Public Park*, the gift of Colonel Blackburn, is situated at the foot of the village.

The Golf Course, $\frac{3}{4}$-mile from the village, on the farm of Drumore, on the Gartness Road, is a very good inland course of 9 holes, from which there is a lovely view all round. There are a good many natural hazards, and the course is steadily improving. It is inclined to be too grassy in autumn, but as the soil is a stiff clay, this usual disadvantage of an inland course is minimised.

George Buchanan's Monument.

The outstanding feature, from a historical point of view, is undoubtedly *George Buchanan's Monument*, erected in 1788. It is a well-proportioned obelisk built of white millstone grit, 19 feet square at the base, 103 feet high, having a cavity which diminishes from 6 feet square at the ground to a point at the height of 54 feet, whence a Norway pole is continued to the top. Killearn is principally known as the birthplace of George Buchanan, poet, historian and reformer. Part of the farmhouse, called the Moss, on the banks of the Blane, in which he was born about February, 1506, remained until 1812, when a modern mansion was built upon the site. In 1570 he was selected for the delicate and responsible position of tutor to His Majesty James VI. He is said to have treated the royal person with such inflexible severity as to make Stirling Castle resound with howls as fervent as ever proceeded from a village dominie's school. While professor of the University of Coimbra, in Portugal, he was thrown into the dungeons of the Inquisition by the Jesuits. He beguiled the weary hours of captivity by writing a Latin paraphrase of the Psalms, much prized for its beauty of simile and felicity of diction. Dryden says, "For the purity of his learning, and for all other endowments belonging to a historian, Buchanan might be placed amongst the greatest. He wrote the history of his country in Latin, and in such Latin as compares with any Roman historian." He died in Edinburgh on Friday, 20th September, 1582, in the 77th year of his age, and was buried in Greyfriars.

The Churches.

The Churches of Killearn are the objects of antiquarian and architectural interest. Killearn village is in the unique position of being at the present time in possession of three Parish Churches—the dismantled ivy-clad pile, the remains of a church rebuilt in 1734, the intermediate barn-like edifice which served from 1826 till 1881, and now utilized as a hall under the management of the Kirk Session, and the present fine place of worship erected by the munificence of the late Sir Archibald Orr-Ewing, Bart., Ballikinrain, in memory of his daughter, Miss Elizabeth Constance Lindsay Orr-Ewing, who died at the early age of 16, and who, by her unaffected piety and noble-minded generosity, won the esteem and sincere affection of all classes. From the historical point of view the old roofless structure will probably, as long as the two other buildings last, command the greatest share of attention. Within its precincts and around it rest the remains not only of the rude forefathers of the beautiful and interesting village, but those of men who have made their names famous in many ways—the Buchanans, the Grahams, the Blackburns, and the Ewings. The churchyard is tended with great care, the ivy-covered walls and closely-cropped turf over and around the graves of the village fathers of generations past and gone suggest such a spot as the poet had in view when he said—

> "But let me lie in a quiet spot with the green
>   turf o'er my head,
> Far from the city's busy hum, the worldling's
>   heavy tread;
> Where the free winds blow, and the branches
>   wave, and the song birds sweetly sing,
> Till every mourner there exclaims,
> 'O Death! where is thy sting.'"

CHURCHYARD AND OLD PARISH CHURCH, KILLEARN.

ADVERTISEMENTS.

BLACK BULL HOTEL,
KILLEARN.

FIRST = CLASS ACCOMMODATION.
Moderate Terms.

GOOD CYCLING ROADS.   GOLF.

D. L. BENNIE,
Proprietor

TELEGRAMS—"HOTEL, KILLEARN."

JOHN M'GREGOR,

KILLEARN,

SMITH AND GENERAL IRONMONGER,

DIP AND OIL MERCHANT.

BEST PARAFFIN OIL STOCKED.

J. & C. BUCHANAN

DRAPERS, HOSIERS, AND

BOOT AND SHOE DEALERS,

Buchanan Street, BALFRON.

Underclothing and Ladies' Outfitting.

Gent.'s Shirts, Collars, Cuffs, Fronts, Ties, Gloves, &c.

Ready-Mades, Waterproofs, and Leggings.

Men's Heavy and Light Nailed Boots.

Ladies' and Gent.'s Glace Kid Boots and Shoes.

Boys' and Girls' Strong and Fine Boots.

The famous "O.K." Boots always in stock.

Canvas Shoes.   Cycling Shoes.

AGENTS FOR W. & J. BOWIE, DYERS.

The *United Free Church* is a neat little edifice, beautifully situated near the entrance to the village from the north. At the time of writing it has been arranged to renovate the whole of the interior of this church.

Other Places of Interest and Mansions.

Blairessan.—Adjoining the village is the farm of Blairessan, on the estate of Carbeth. Near the Spouthead of Blairessan tradition asserts a bloody battle was fought between the Romans and the Scots. Formerly several large stones indicated the supposed scene of the fray.

Leaving the village by the road opposite the Old Toll House, and proceeding in a south-westerly direction, the visitor will be struck with the magnificent view in front. About ¾ of a mile beyond Killearn Station is *Killearn House*, situated on the banks of the Blane. Mr. John Blackburn, merchant, Glasgow, purchased Killearn estate from Sir James Montgomery in 1812. In 1829 he also bought Croy Leckie, and built the present house there. The old house of Killearn, belonging to the Grahams, occupied a site in the Place Parks, still easily found near the village. The late Mr. Peter Blackburn, Chairman of the Edinburgh and Glasgow Railway and some time M.P. for Stirlingshire, and the late Lord Blackburn, the eminent judge, were sons of Mr. John Blackburn, who purchased the estate. The present proprietor is Lieutenant-Colonel Blackburn, Royal Artillery.

Finnich Glen, close by Killearn House, is a rocky

ravine, nearly 100 feet in depth, and in places not more than 10 feet wide, between whose overhanging walls flows a tortuous stream—the Carnock. The ravine, at most parts impassable, may be entered and viewed either at its lower or upper end, and presents a wild and romantic picture. The bottom is reached at the upper end by a flight of stone steps—78 in number—partly cut and partly built in a crevice of the rock. A somewhat ticklish pathway leads to a mass of rock known as the "Deil's Pulpit," where only moonlight is wanted to produce the most weird and awesome effect. The overhanging rocks have a grandeur and sublimity of aspect that fill the mind of the beholder with awe and admiration, and this feeling is increased by the intense solitude, and a natural, healthy sense of personal insignificance.

Aucheneck House lies a short distance to the east of Finnich Glen. Aucheneck estate belongs to Mrs. John Wilson, widow of the late Mr. John Wilson, India merchant. It is picturesquely situated, and from the top of the Caldon Hill the view of the surrounding district is unrivalled. Traces are to be found here of the numerous chapels once dedicated to the blessed Kessog, the patron saint of the old Earls of Lennox.

Some three miles in a south-easterly direction from Aucheneck is the *Whangie*, on the opposite side of Auchineden Hill, approached from Auchineden Lodge. On descending the hill, the storm-beaten rocks of the Whangie soon become apparent. This singular chasm or cleft, looks as if a part of the hill had been cut or chopped off, hence the name "Whangie," and every-

POT OF GARTNESS.

one familiar with the Scottish tongue, knows that a whang means a slice, as a slice of bread or cheese. When the Highlanders raided the Lennox the recesses of the Whangie were used for concealing cattle; and after the defeat of the Highlanders at Culloden, proscribed Jacobites found shelter here from the bloodhounds of Cumberland.

Pot of Gartness.

Fully a mile from the village of Killearn, in a westerly direction, is the well-known *Pot of Gartness* It consists of a series of rocky pools and terraces in the river Endrick, where, on a September afternoon, it is interesting to watch the salmon in their persevering and bold attempts to mount the barrier. This is a sight which no visitor should miss. The caldron-shaped cavity, the picturesque cataract, and enchanting surroundings form a picture not soon to be forgotten. The "Pot" at times literally boils with fish.

John Napier of Merchiston, the celebrated inventor of logarithms, during a considerable part of the period employed in his calculations, resided at the house of Gartness, near the romantic cascade. Hume has said of Napier that "he was the person to whom the title of 'Great Man' is more justly due than to any other whom his country has produced." Local tradition claims Drumbeg, then a lowly thatched farmhouse in the parish of Drymen, as his birth-place, while Balfron points to Edenbellie. It is to be feared, however, that a better claim can be substantiated, and that the distinction must be given to Merchiston Castle, near

Edinburgh. It was said that the incessant noise made by the fall of water at the Pot of Gartness did not disturb Napier in his studies, but that the clatter of the neighbouring mill so distracted his meditations that he was frequently obliged to request the miller to stop the wheel. Accustomed frequently to walk out in the evening in his nightgown and cap, and wearing an aspect of deep abstraction, he obtained the reputation among the people of being a warlock. Fragments of the ruins of the castle in which he lived are to be seen overhanging the falls of Gartness, and a stone, with the date 1574, taken from the ruins, is built into the gable of the mill. Napier was born in 1550 and died 1617.

Drymen.

DRYMEN is derived from the Celtic word Druim, a ridge or knoll. The numerous knolls throughout the parish lend support to this explanation of the name, formerly written Drumen, and the present local pronunciation accords with this old spelling It is also said that the name originated at a meeting called for the purpose of giving a name to the parish. After prolonged deliberation, with no practical result, one of the party left in disgust, accusing the others of being a lot of *dry men.* It is too apparent, however, that this is one of those fairy tales invented to account for an interesting name. The population of the parish in 1891 was 1512, and in 1901, 1390.

The Village.

The village of Drymen, with a population of 340, is about a mile north from the Endrick, 1½ miles in the same direction from the station, and 16 miles from Glasgow.

It consists of a number of houses on the four roads converging upon the square locally known as the "Cross Green," and of a fringe of houses on each side of the green. It is a quiet, quaint place, with various bright modern features. It possesses a Parish Church, a U.F Church, Public Hall, Library and Reading Room, and a branch of the Royal Bank of Scotland.

The Parish Church is a plain, substantial edifice, built in 1771, and seated for 600. In 1879 both exterior and interior were improved, and again in 1898 further extension was rendered necessary. Both of these alterations and improvements were largely due to the exertions of the Rev. John Roy, M.A., the minister of the parish.

One of the principal landmarks of the parish, the *Bell Tree*, stood in the churchyard beside the gate. It was an immense ash tree, supposed to be 300 or 400 years old. In May, 1899, it girthed 17 feet $5\frac{1}{2}$ inches at 1 foot from the ground, and 17 feet $4\frac{1}{2}$ inches at 5 feet from the ground. The church bell, which summoned the parishioners to worship, used to hang on one of its branches. This tree was blown down by a gale of wind, on 23rd September, 1892, to the great regret of the good people of Drymen.

The U.F. Church, built in 1819, stands on the north side of the Stirling Road. The Rev Andrew Wilson, M.A., has efficiently ministered to this congregation for the period of 45 years. An interesting stone, built into the porch of this church above the entrance, bears the inscription, "Christ is Head over all His Body, the Church." This stone was originally placed over the doorway of a little building at the back of Duncryne Hill, Kilmaronock, where the congregation worshipped for a time after its formation near the close of the eighteenth century. In the early years of the last century it was decided to make Drymen their headquarters, and on taking leave of the old church they took the stone which set forth their ecclesiastical principles out of the wall and carried it with them. Placed for safety under the pulpit of the new church, it remained hidden for 70 years, until brought to light again, about 18 years ago, when the church was being repaired, and was built in over the door of the porch, which was then under construction. This is an example of the strength of principle which animated the founders of the Secession Churches of the district.

The *Public School* is prettily situated about half-a-mile east of the village on the Stirling Road.

A fine *Golf Course*, with a well-appointed clubhouse, situated on the lands of Drumbeg, and adjoining the historic Drymen Bridge, now forms an additional attraction to the neighbourhood.

Visitors to the village of Drymen should not miss the view to be had from an eminence locally known as the *Backhill*, nearly opposite the Buchanan Arms Hotel. In the foreground you look down upon the rich and extensive lawn of Buchanan, studded with innumerable trees; beyond there is Loch Lomond, with Ben Leven and the mountains of Argyle in the background.

For many years *Drymen Feeing Fair*, held in the Square twice a year, in May and November, was one of the most popular gatherings in Strathendrick, but like other institutions of a similar kind, it has been shorn of its former glory. Forty years ago, not only the Square, but the roads leading to it, were crowded with rosy-cheeked lasses and athletic lads, bent on making a day of it. The elements of amusement were abundant. There were shooting galleries, where whoever wished might try his skill, and gain no end of hollow nuts for his pains, and sweety stalls were conspicuous, where the rustic swain treated with lavish hand, and no particular discrimination, the sturdy and festive damsels, who, in anticipation of numerous "fairings," had each provided herself with a bag, or a number of extensive handkerchiefs. But the most attractive feature of the fair was the "penny reel." Dancing to the strains of Geordie "Blaw's" fiddle was a luxury eagerly looked forward to by the streams of giddy gallants that poured into the Square.

Notable Personages.

The Drummonds.—The noble family of Drummond derive their name from this parish. Their origin is traditionally traced to a nobleman of Hungary, named Maurice, who accompanied Edgar Atheling and his two sisters to Scotland in 1068 when they fled from the hostilities of William the Conqueror. The vessel carrying the Royal fugitives, and piloted by this Maurice, was cast by stress of weather upon the coast of Fife. They were received with kindness, and hospitably entertained by Malcolm Canmore, who married Margaret, the elder of the two princesses, and conferred on the Hungarian Maurice, among other possessions, Drymen or Druiman, whence his descendants took their surname. It is not known when the residence of the Drummonds was transferred to Stobhall, Perthshire; but previous to this Arabella, daughter of Sir John Drummond, married in 1357

ADVERTISEMENTS.

GEORGE GILFILLAN,

Bootmaker and General Draper,

HILLSIDE,

ESTABLISHED 60 YEARS.   DRYMEN.

My BOOTS, SHOES, AND SLIPPERS ARE WELL-SELECTED AND RELIABLE.

Anything not in Stock in DRAPERY or BOOTS, &c., can be got or Made to Measure in a Few Days.

DAVID WILKIE,

Grocer, Draper, and General Merchant,

HOPE HOUSE,

DRYMEN.

TAILORING in all its Branches.
OILSKINS, WATERPROOF CAPES and COATS.
CYCLES and CYCLE ACCESSORIES Supplied.
Agent for Hand and Family SEWING MACHINES.

Articles not stocked supplied with the least possible delay.

ADVERTISEMENTS.

Buchanan Arms Hotel,
DRYMEN.

FIRST=CLASS FAMILY, TOURIST, AND COMMERCIAL HOTEL.

SITUATED AMID MAGNIFICENT SCENERY.

Parties Booked by Week, Month, or Week End.

POSTING IN ALL ITS BRANCHES.

GOLF COURSE within 10 Minutes' Walk, and Excellent TROUT FISHING on Endrick within same distance.

JAMES BUCHANAN, Proprietor.

THE SQUARE, DRYMEN.

John, Earl of Carrick, High Steward of Scotland, afterwards Robert the Third, and thus became Queen of Scotland, and the mother of David, Duke of Rothesay, who was cruelly starved to death in the palace of Falkland in 1402, and of James the First. Drymen has reason to be proud of having produced a lady from whom descended the Royal House of Stewart, and who, owing to the deficiencies of her husband, was compelled to take an active part in the management of the State, which she did with eminent prudence and success.

The Rev. Duncan Macfarlan, a muscular divine, who died in 1791, had to resort to physical force to quell the disorders which invariably took place at these gatherings. Fights between Drymen and Gartmore people on account of some injury, or supposed injury, were frequent. Mr. Macfarlan's emblem of peace and wand of office, or pastoral staff, was a stout stick or rung, and for the excellent use he made of it, he was called and is known to posterity as Duncan "Rungs."

The Rev. Duncan Macfarlan, D.D., a son of Duncan "Rungs," was born in Drymen manse, 27th September, 1771, and succeeded his father as minister of the parish before he was 20 years of age. In 1806 he received the degree of Doctor of Divinity from the University of Glasgow; in 1810 the same University elected him Dean of Faculties. In 1815 he was appointed one of His Majesty's chaplains for Scotland, and in 1819 was elected Moderator of the General Assembly. Though the minister of Drymen was thus much occupied with educational and ecclesiastical matters outwith his parish, he never neglected his parochial duties, and when in April, 1823, he was appointed Principal of the University of Glasgow, and minister of the High Church, both in succession to the Rev. Dr. Taylor, the parish of Drymen parted with him with much regret. For nearly thirty-five years thereafter he managed the affairs of the University with tact and success, and his services to the Church of Scotland during these critical years, including his second Moderatorship in 1843, were of the utmost importance. Few ministers of the Church of Scotland have been held in higher esteem He died in 1857, and a very imposing monument has been erected to his memory in the Glasgow Necropolis.

The Rev. Alexander Lochore, D.D., for 53 years, from 1824 till 1877, passed a singularly peaceful, useful, and honoured life as minister of the parish. Dr. Lochore was looked up to as a model of what a Christian gentleman should be.

Rambles around Drymen.

About 300 yards from the Parish Church on the Glasgow Road, on the right, is the principal entrance to Buchanan Castle, the seat of the Duke of Montrose. There are several other entrances in Buchanan and Kilmaronock. (See pages 80 and 90).

Just beyond, within a mile of the village, is *Drymen Bridge*, crossing the Endrick, and connecting the parish with that of Kilmaronock. This bridge, built in 1765, is reputed to be the finest that spans the Endrick. From the bridge down to the mouth of the Endrick there is a fine stretch of level land dotted with clumps of trees, with the Endrick meandering through it, and the Luss Hills forming a background. This stretch of ground is known as the "Haughs" of the Endrick.

Dalnair, a fine castellated mansion, stands on the south side of the River Endrick, near Drymen Station. The estate and house formely known as Endrickbank were purchased in 1883 by Mr. Thomas Brown from the trustees of Mr. Charles H. H Wilsone. The old house was taken down shortly after, and the present handsome residence built by Mr. Brown.

Proceeding along the Glasgow Road, from above and below Finnich Toll, a magnificent prospect presents itself, which amply repays a visit. At your feet lies the modern mansion-house of Dalnair, whilst east and west stretches far, the fair valley of Endrick, with Loch Lomond in the distance.

Finnich Glen, 3 miles from Drymen, see page 63.

Returning to the village of Drymen, and taking the Drumfrosk Road towards Gartness and Killearn, a stretch of land is passed sloping down towards the west, which would make the laird's fortune if it were within reach of a populous centre. It is sheltered on the east, and looks down to Loch Lomond. On this road, a mile and a half on the right, is an old house called the *Park of Drumquhassle*, which is said to have sheltered Prince Charlie. The house belongs to the Govane family, who formerly owned much of the land round about.

Gateside, standing near the Gartness Road, about half-a-mile east of the village, is a modern house belonging to Mr. Archibald M. Macqueen, of London, and used by him as a summer residence. Mr. Macqueen is the son of a former schoolmaster of the parish.

Pot of Gartness (2 miles), see page 65.

The Old Drove Road that leads northward from Drymen over the hill to Gartmore is an ideal one for the pedestrian, though unfit for vehicles The view from this road is most enchanting, the strath is seen from end to end, Gartmore stands opposite on the slope of a hill, and there are also seen the valleys of Loch Ard and Menteith, the fertile carse of Stirling, the Wallace Monument, and Gartincaber Tower, near Doune. The view thus obtained amply rewards a rather toilsome 3 mile walk to the summit of the hill, which we may mention forms part of the watershed of the Clyde and Forth. On the way the visitor cannot fail to notice the desolate character of the surroundings. The little loch near the summit of the hill is reserved for private fishing by His Grace, the Duke of Montrose. When Mr. Wilkes and his friend Churchhill visited Scotland about 1760, they were so horrified with the appearance of this wilderness that they thought they had reached the utmost bound of Scottish cultivation. They turned their horses, and sought shelter at Buchanan House, where, in the absence of the Duke, they were most hospitably entertained for three days.

The satirical poet on reaching London returned the hospitality by writing his celebrated poem entitled, "The Prophecy of Famine," in which he introduces the scene of Drymen Muir. The lines referred to were written in 1763, and begin as follows—

"Far as the eye could reach no trace was seen,
　Earth clothed in russet, scorned the lively green.
　The plague of locusts they secure defy,
　For in three hours a grasshopper must die.
　No living thing, whate'er its food, feasts there
　But the cameleon who can feast on air,
　No birds, except as birds of passage, flew,
　No bee was known to hum, no dove to coo,
　No streams as amber smooth, as amber clear,
　Were seen to glide, or heard to warble here."

Going east by the Stirling Road, about a quarter of a mile from the village on the right hand side, is passed a slightly rising piece of ground which is known as the *Castle Hill*, and on the other side of the road, 200 yards to the north, there is a wood known as the *Gallows Hill*. Who lived in the castle and who used the gallows nobody seems to know. The names scarcely suggest forgotten history. During the eighteenth century a Sheriff Court was held in Drymen for the trial of smugglers and other minor delinquents, and possibly the gallows may then have been in full swing.

The *Altquhar* (locally Urwhurr) *Burn* rising in the hill behind the historic house of Craigievairn (*i.e.*, water rock) flows through a beautiful glen, which, however, is not easily traversed, and crosses the Stirling Road 1½ miles east of the village, after which, passing between the farms of Blairnavaid and Blairo'er, Drumquhassle and Gartacharn and through the farm of Dalnair, empties its waters at length into the Endrick. The glen is perhaps most picturesque at Craigievairn, where there are some fine old trees and a pretty waterfall   Here again we are on historic ground. Near the present Craigievairn house stood at one time *Craigievairn Castle*, the home of the Buchanans of that ilk, while on the opposite side of the glen stood the Blairfad Meal and Lint Mill, which, however, has been idle for over forty years. There was a castle here also, but no visible traces of these ancient castles are now to be found, although a field in front of Craigievairn still bears the name of the Castle Field. Recollections of this glen inspired a Drymen man, separated from the scenes of his youth, to write:—

> " 'Twas there in boyhood's early days,
> I gathered hazel nuts and slaes;
> Fond memory ponders o'er the scene,
> Though many years have rolled between.
>
> The burn, embosomed in the glen,
> Each ferny nook and bosky den,
> My fav'rite haunts, I roamed at will,
> In fancy I can see them still."

A mile further east, on the right, is Balfunning, the mansion of Mr. John Fraser.

About a mile from this, taking the first road on the right and thereafter the first on the left, is Balfron Station. By keeping to the Stirling Road for a short distance the *Bog of Ballat* is reached. With an elevation of only 222 feet above the level of the sea, this forms the summit line between the east coast and west coast of Scotland.

Buchanan.

According to the Rev. J. B. Johnston, author of "Place Names of Scotland," Buchanan is derived from the Gaelic "bogh chanan," "low ground belonging to the canon," or perhaps more correctly belonging to the canonist. It was formerly spelt Bouchannane.

Buchanan is a territorial surname very common in Strathendrick. The founder of the family was Anselan, son of O'Kyan, King of Ulster, in Ireland, who landed in this country in 1016, married the heiress of the lands of Buchanan, which afterwards became the family name. Besides the M'Aslans, which is a corruption of Anselan, the founder, the Buchanans recognise as clansmen the Yuils and Risks, originally mere soubriquets of individuals, but afterwards the surname of their descendants. The one was called from the day of his birth, Yule (Christmas); the other from the place of his residence, the Risk (a bare knoll) of Drymen.

The parish, a somewhat extensive one, measuring $18\frac{1}{2}$ miles long, with a width varying from $2\frac{1}{4}$ to 6 miles, is the property of the Duke of Montrose, the noble representative of a gallant line whose fame equals its antiquity. His Grace is the twenty-first lineal descendant of Sir Patrick de Graham, who was killed at the battle of Dunbar in 1296, and mourned by friend and foe. The Grahams have been distinguished for their military achievements, Sir John de Graham, who fell in the battle of Falkirk, was the companion and beloved friend of Wallace; the

Marquis of Montrose was a conspicuous leader during the civil wars; Viscount Dundee fell in a brave but vain endeavour to support the tottering cause of James II.; and Thomas Graham, afterwards Lord Lynedoch, distinguished himself by his heroic conduct in the war of the French Revolution. Of the latter it was said, "Never was there seated a loftier spirit in a brave heart." The present Duke, who is a generous landlord, and deservedly popular in the district, is Lord Register of Scotland and Lord Lieutenant of the County of Stirling. At the time of writing he commands a battalion of the Argyll and Sutherland Highlanders in the South African War.

From Drymen to Balmaha.

The road from Drymen to Balmaha affords a charming walk. Till it reaches the Milton it skirts on the left for a distance of 2½ miles the beautifully-wooded ducal policies.

Buchanan Castle, the residence of the Duke of Montrose, is a mile west of Drymen village. The old mansion-house having been destroyed by fire in 1850, the present building was completed in 1857. At the death of the last Buchanan of that ilk in 1682, the estate was sold by his executors to the family of Montrose. The castle is a handsome structure, the grounds extensive and well wooded, some of the trees being remarkable specimens of their kind.

A row of houses with a profusion of flowers growing in front are tenanted by the Duke's workmen.

Buchanan has no village, but the church and school,

DRYMEN BRIDGE.

with a few cottages at the roadside at the Milton, form the clachan of the parish. *The Church,* which was built in the latter half of the eighteenth century, is neat and well kept, and is seated for 214. The gallery is reserved for the Montrose family.

Buchanan Churchyard contains a number of stones belonging to Buchanan of Auchmar. It is questionable, however, if any of the Auchmars are buried here. When the present church was built permission was given to the last representative of the Auchmars to remove the stones from the burying-place of the chapel near the Duke's stables, and where the Montrose family now have their place of sepulture. The late Marquis of Graham, elder brother of the present Duke, is interred at a spot opposite the western door of the church. This young nobleman contracted fever while visiting Rome, and died in England at the age of 25. In accordance with his own request his remains rest in this quiet spot.

The School of Buchanan was ruled for the long period of 40 years by Charles Macphie, as he was affectionately called, born at Balfron, 31st December, 1813, and who died here, 29th November, 1890.

St. Maha's Well is on the farm of Creitichall. It used to be resorted to by pilgrims in need of healing in those dark ages of sanitary and medical science. Pieces of cloth were hung on an overhanging tree, and the good offices of the saint invoked by votive offerings Balmaha retains the same name, which probably refers to St. Maha of Kingarth in Bute.

A short distance to the right of the road is the manse, built in 1797, overlooking Loch Lomond. The original manse was situated on the bank of the loch opposite Inchcailloch.

Balmaha is fully 4 miles from Drymen. From here a splendid view of the wooded islands of Loch Lomond is obtainable.

The *Montrose Holiday Home* for poor children was erected by the Duchess of Montrose in 1891. The building is of two storeys, plain but neat, and commands a charming stretch of the loch. The home was devised to enable children from the more congested parts of Glasgow to enjoy "the fresh-air fortnight." Her Grace, who presides over this institution, is best known in the West of Scotland for her benevolence and active charity.

A manufactory for the production of pyroligneous acid is carried on at Balmaha. All kinds of hard wood are used, but particularly oak.

Balmaha Pier is one of the places of call for the Loch Lomond steamers.

Inchcailloch (Island of the Nun) is almost within a stone-throw from the Pier. It is 7 furlongs in length and $3\frac{1}{2}$ furlongs in breadth, and for beauty of form and wealth of verdant apparel, it is surpassed by no other isle on Loch Lomond To every dweller on the "Bonnie Banks of Loch Lomond" Inchcailloch is sacred as the place where the early worshippers heard the Gospel sound, and where the rude forefathers of the district sleep. Inchcailloch gave the name to the parish until the middle of the seventeenth century, when it was altered to Buchanan. The church on this island, used as the Parish Church till 1621, was built in 1170 over the grave of St. Kentigerna, who came to the island about the end of the 7th century. This church seems to have been of great beauty, as evidenced by recent excavations.

A little to the north-east *Conic Hill* (1176) is conspicuous, a characteristic of which is the almost total absence of snow when the surrounding hills are clothed in white.

The Pass of Balmaha is at the entrance to the road passing along the shores of the loch toward Rowardennan. The Pass is regarded at this point as the key to the Highlands, where

> "A hundred men might hold the post
> With hardihood against the host."

In the days gone by the lawless tribes of the Loch Lomond country gushed through the Pass like a mountain torrent upon the peaceful plains below. The road winds away along the side of the Loch to Rowardennan (6 miles), from which Ben Lomond (3192 feet), famous in song and story, can be ascended; and for other two miles, when it terminates at Ptarmigan Shooting Lodge, whence only a bridle path leads to Inversnaid, six miles beyond. From Inversnaid the distance to Stronaclachar, on Loch Katrine, is 5 miles. At the back of Inversnaid Hotel the Arklet Water, pouring over a precipitous rock, forms the well-known Falls of Inversnaid, while a mile from the hotel are the remains of a fort and garrison built in 1713 to repress the predatory Highlanders, and more especially the Macgregors. It is an interesting fact that the hero of Quebec, General Wolfe, when a subaltern, did duty here.

Kilmaronock.

SEVERAL definitions have been given of the name of the parish of Kilmaronock, but the most obvious is *Kil-ma-Ronach*, the Kirk of St. Ronach. St. Ronach was a famous missionary priest of the early church, St. Ronan, who tarried here for a time on his journey from Kilmarnock, in Ayrshire, to Kilmaronaig, on Loch Etive, in order to propagate the Gospel among the wild inhabitants. St. Ronan's Well, on the lands of Mains, west of the Parish Church, still preserves the saint's name intact.

The parish is near the centre of Dumbartonshire, on the southern shore of Loch Lomond. For five miles the Endrick threads its tortuous way through the fertile land, forming the boundary line between Stirlingshire and Dumbartonshire, and discharging its waters into Loch Lomond, opposite the island of Clarinch, whose name was once the slogan of the Clan Buchanan.

Though little more than 20 miles from the heart of Glasgow, the district remains almost as little visited as if it were in Shetland. The population of the parish in 1901 was 874.

From Caldarvan Station.

Starting from *Caldarvan Station*, on the Forth and Clyde Railway, and proceeding in the direction of the hamlet of Gartocharn, about 8 minutes walk takes the visitor to *Auchenlarich*, nicely seated on a hill on the left, the residence of Mr. George Eyre-Todd, the well-known author and editor of Scottish works.

Caldarvan House, the residence of Mr. R. D. Mackenzie, is beautifully placed on the rising ground 2 miles from the station, and half-a-mile above the village. Mr. Mackenzie was formerly head of the firm of Mackenzie, Gardner & Alexander, writers, Glasgow. He was for many years Convener of the County of Dumbarton, and was the first Chairman of the County Council. Much of the beauty of the middle part of Kilmaronock is due to plantations judiciously formed by him. Among these plantations Caldarvan Loch, a sheet of water of about 30 acres, has been well stocked with Loch Leven trout.

The hamlet, or village of *Gartocharn*, 2½ miles from the station, and about a mile from the shores of Loch Lomond, is situated on a slope, commanding a charming prospect of water, wood, and girdling hill. This is just such a spot as would delight the heart of a Ruskin or a Blackie, removed as it is from the modern aggression of steam.

It was here that the luckless Earl of Argyle's expedition came to grief in 1685. The incident is related in Macaulay's History. In the hope of overthrowing the government of James VII., he had landed on the shores of Loch Fyne, collected his clan, and marched for Glasgow. Crossing the Leven at Balloch, he had reached the little stream here, when he found the village occupied by the royal troops. An attack would probably have been successful, but he was induced to turn aside and cross the hills. It was a dark night, and amid the bogs on the moors most of his men deserted. At Kilpatrick, in the morning, only 500 men answered to their names, and the Earl gave up his attempt. He was captured an hour or two later, attempting to escape across the Clyde at Blytheswood. "Unhappy Argyle!"

The United Free Church stands here. The congregation worshipping in this church was originally formed in 1772, and was connected with the Relief Synod. At the union of the Secession and Relief Churches in 1847, the congregation became United Presbyterian, and subsequently by the union of the Free and United Presbyterian Churches it became the United Free. The original church was replaced by a new one in 1854. The present minister, the Rev. James Dunlop, has faithfully and successfully ministered to this congregation for 50 years.

To the west of Gartocharn, *Duncryne*, a larch-covered hill, rising from the middle of the parish to a height of 450 feet, is a striking and beautiful feature of the landscape. The magnificent scenery of the surrounding country, redolent of romantic associations, is seen to advantage from the summit of this hill. To the west, overlooking the shore of Loch Lomond between Balloch and the Ross, is Mount Misery, at some parts rising to a height of 800 or 900 feet. Beyond this appear the hills of Cardross and Row, and in the distance the bold mountain-tops of Cowal. To the north lies Loch Lomond, fairest of scenes, beautifully gemmed with wooded islands, and screened by rugged mountains, conspicuous among them being the lofty Ben Lomond. On the east and towards the south lies the valley of the Endrick, with a rich and varied background of

> "Mountains that like giants stand
> To sentinel enchanted land,"

from the distant Ochils to the neighbouring Kilpatrick Hills; while in the south-west are unmistakable signs of the busy industry of the Vale of Leven, with Dumbarton and Dumbarton Castle at the further end.

On a rising ground, half-a-mile from Loch Lomond, stands *Boturich Castle*, built on part of the ruin of an ancient castle of the same name, which belonged to the Haldanes of Gleneagles, and seems to have been a magnificent edifice. This is the seat of Mr. R. E. Findlay, of the firm of Richardson, Findlay & Co., merchants, Glasgow.

Ross Priory.

Midway along the shore of Loch Lomond, occupying the crest of a gentle rising ground, amid oaks and beeches, is *Ross Priory*, the residence of Sir George H. Leith-Buchanan, Bart.

Through openings among the branches of its trees the windows look to the east and west—to Ross-dhu, the ancestral seat of the Colquhouns, on the western shore near Luss, and to Buchanan Castle, eastward beyond the Endrick, the residence of the Duke of Montrose. As the name suggests, this was at one time a religious house. The Buchanans who owned and occupied it, were the Buchanans of Drumakill at Drymen, the same branch as that from which the distinguished George Buchanan sprang, and descended from a daughter of King Robert III.

After the Rebellion of 1745 a strange incident occurred here. One of the Macgregors in full flight before the "red soldiers" sought the protection of the laird, who received the fugitive with demonstrations of sympathy and friendship, and leading him to a room in the upper part of the house, locked the door, assuring him of his safety. His pursuers, immediately following, demanded of the laird if he had seen the Macgregor, and tradition says that Buchanan betrayed his guest, and so violated the laws of hospitality. When the prisoner was being dragged away he is said to have turned round, and with a fierce look of hate, hurled the curse prophetic at Buchanan, "There'll be Macgregors on the braes of Balquhidder when there's ne'er a Buchanan at the Ross!" Whether we believe in Highland "second-sight" or not, it is curious that the family of Buchanan has disappeared, male heirs having failed, and Ross Priory passed through a daughter of the house into the line of its present owner.

In the time of Sir Walter Scott, the owner of the Ross was Mr. Hector Macdonald, an Edinburgh advocate, who had married the heiress of the last of the Buchanans. Lockhart, Sir Walter's biographer, refers to Macdonald as "a frank and generous gentleman, and not the less acceptable to Scott for the Highland prejudices he inherited with the high blood of Clanranald, at whose beautiful seat of Ross Priory, on

MAINS CASTLE, KILMARONOCK.

the shore of Loch Lomond, he was almost annually a visitor—a circumstance which has left many traces in the 'Waverley Novels.' Tradition points to a certain room in Ross Priory as that in which Scott wrote the noble boat-song, "Roderich vich Alpine Dhu." The scene of the great victory of the Macgregors over the Colquhouns is visible, just across the loch, from the windows—

> "Proudly our pibroch has thrilled in Glen Fruin,
> And Bannochar's groans to our slogan replied;
> Glen Luss and Ross-dhu, they are smoking in ruin,
> And the best of Loch Lomond lie dead on her side.
> Widow and Saxon maid
> Long shall lament our raid,
> Think of Clan-Alpine with fear and with woe;
> Lennox and Leven-glen
> Shake when they hear agen
> Roderich vich Alpine dhu, ho! ieroe!"

By wrapping himself in the hide of "the white bull of Gallingad," Brian the hermit procured the augury which cost Roderich his life. Scott's description of the animal might fill breeders of stock for the show-ring with despair—

> "His hide was snow, his horns were dark,
> His red eye glowed like fiery spark."

It has been pointed out as a proof of Scott's painstaking care in detail and local colour, that the farm of Gallingad, in the parish of Kilmaronock, is still famous for its breed of cattle. The estate was recently purchased from Mr. Cunninghame-Graham of Gartmore by Mr. Christie of Levenfield, one of the Turkey-red manufacturers of the Vale of Leven,

From Gartocharn to Drymen.

Leaving Gartocharn by the east, about $2\frac{1}{2}$ miles distant on the left is the *Parish Church*. This church was built in 1813, and has 400 sittings. The present minister, the Rev. Wm. Boyd, M.A., was elected assistant and successor to the late Rev. W. B. S. Paterson in 1879.

On the same side, 200 yards further along, is the entrance to the ruinous *Castle of Mains*, which is of very ancient date. "Over an arched window of the building there is still to be seen a lozenge-shaped shield, charged with a bend dexter, the bearing of the Dennistouns of that ilk, from whom the property passed into the hands of the first Earl of Dundonald. This roofless, time-gnawed, lofty square keep, which wears a plume of trees upon its crest, is an imposing object in the district." The Dundonald family sold the Mains with the Castle to the ancestors of the late Mr. Robert M'Goune, from whom it passed into the possession of Mr. John Robert Bruce Macadam, and is now the property of Mr. John Macadam, banker, Balfron, who has built a handsome and tasteful residence close beside it.

Following this road eastward for about half-a-mile, on the right is *Catter House*, the residence of Mr. W. W. Murray, chamberlain to the Duke of Montrose. This fine old mansion commands a full view of the lawn and wooded pleasure-grounds of Buchanan Castle.

There is a large artificial earthen mound here,

anciently the seat of justice and the scene of executions. When the neighbouring district was granted to Malise, Chief of Buchanan, in 1285, the Earl of Lennox reserved to himself the right of execution of persons condemned by the Chief on the Gallows Hill of Catter. Near this the Earl of Lennox had a residence, but time has done its work so effectually that no trace of it is now to be found. In Bruce's time the old Earl of Lennox, or Levenax (the ancient name of Loch Lomond was Loch Leven), was one of the most devoted adherents of the struggling King.

A short distance from Catter, the road joins the highway from Glasgow to Drymen. By this highway, taking to the left, and passing over *Drymen Bridge*, which unites the parishes of Kilmaronock and Drymen, the village of Drymen is reached in about a mile, while to the right lies the hamlet of *Croftamie* and Drymen Station on the Forth and Clyde Railway.

Buchlyvie.

BUCHLYVIE, situated midway between Balfron and Kippen, is a tidy, healthy village, stretching along the Dumbarton and Stirling Road, on an eminence commanding a splendid view of Ben Lomond, Ben Venue, Ben Ledi, and the Menteith Hills. From Culbowie Road, which leads southwards from the village, the view obtained can hardly be surpassed. As a heading to the 28th chapter of "Rob Roy" Sir Walter Scott quotes the following old Scottish rhyme—

> "Baron o' Buchlyvie,
> May the foul fiend drive ye,
> And a' tae pieces rive ye,
> For biggin' sic a toon,
> Whaur there's neither horse meat
> Nor man's meat, nor a chair to sit doon."

This personage, so adversely criticised and distinguished, was Sir Andrew Graham, second son of the Marquis of Montrose, and who is said to have founded the present village as far back as 1680. The population is 320. There are two churches, an Established and a United Free, the latter being one of the most interesting edifices in the district. It was built by the Associate Seceeders in 1751 at the modest cost of £153 5s. It must be borne in mind, however, that zeal for the church was a much more prominent feature

ADVERTISEMENTS.

THE RED LION HOTEL,

BUCHLYVIE.

Conducted by Present Family for over 33 Years.

COMMERCIAL, TOURIST, and FAMILY.

SPECIAL RATES TO MEMBERS OF THE SCOTTISH CYCLISTS' UNION.

POSTING.

PURE AND BRACING ATMOSPHERE.

Surrounding District scene of the exploits of Rob Roy.

PARTIES CATERED FOR.

Mrs. M'CALLUM, *Proprietrix.*

ADVERTISEMENTS.

Telegraphic Address—
"M'PHIE, BUCHLYVIE."

ESTABLISHED 1850.

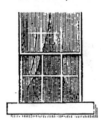
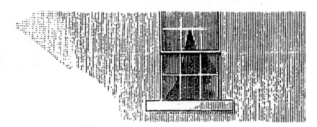
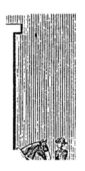

James M'Phie & Son,
WHOLESALE AND RETAIL
Family Grocers, Grain & Provision Merchants,
IRONMONGERS,
BOOT AND SHOE DEALERS,
~ BUCHLYVIE.

Try Our Famed 1/10 TEA.

of those days than of ours, and that all the necessary materials were brought from far and near free of cost by the members. The building is plain even to severity, yet presents quite a picturesque appearance as it stands in the centre of the old graveyard. The original walls, covered by the old roof, remain, but the interior was renovated and reconstructed in 1890, principally through the energy of the late Rev. James Berry, a devoted and respected minister of this congregation for 39 years.

Buchlyvie people are naturally proud of their *Public Hall*, which occupies a prominent position at the western end of the village, and its shapely tower can be seen from many points miles distant. This building was erected in 1884, chiefly through the munificence of a native of Buchlyvie, the late Mr. Alexander Harvie, of the well-known firm, Harvie & M'Gavin, grain merchants, Glasgow.

In recent years Buchlyvie has been famous for its annual ploughing match, held under the auspices of Buchlyvie Ploughing Society. There are open and confined classes, and hundreds gather, not only from the surrounding district, but also from considerable distances to witness the competitions.

Garry's Hole (or, otherwise, *Garry's Den*) lies to the south of the village, at the side of the burn. It is cut out of the solid rock, and, piercing the braeface for a number of feet, has at least three turnings. Tradition says that Garry's Den was used by the Covenanters as a refuge and hiding place from their persecutors, and also by the M'Gregors when on plundering expeditions.

Leaving Buchlyvie by the East.

Following the road eastwards from the village *The Fairy Knowe* stands to the south of Mains Farm. This knowe, or knoll, is said to have been used as a Druidical temple. It is some 40 yards in diameter. About 220 yards to the north is pointed out the place where once stood the Castle of the Baron of Buchlyvie, and where he exercised "the law of pit and gallows."

Proceeding along the road *Garden* is passed on the left. Rob Roy made frequent visits to this mansion. Mr. James Stirling, the proprietor, is the lineal representative of a brave and patriotic race, which has held Garden estate for about 200 years.

Arngibbon Glen, on Garden estate, is one of the loveliest of Scottish glens. Within its recesses the geologist may freely explore, the botanist roam at large, and the lover of nature find instruction in his leisure. It is 2 miles in length, with several waterfalls, the first being half-a-mile up, for which distance there is a well kept path.

On the opposite side of the road there is *Arngibbon*, the ancient seat of the Forresters of that ilk, a doughty clan whose deeds shine fair in the annals of our national history.

Arnprior.

The hamlet of Arnprior is $2\frac{1}{4}$ miles from Buchlyvie. The Castle, the residence of the "king of Kippen," stood on the banks of the burn a few yards above the Mill. The spot can still be pointed out, although no

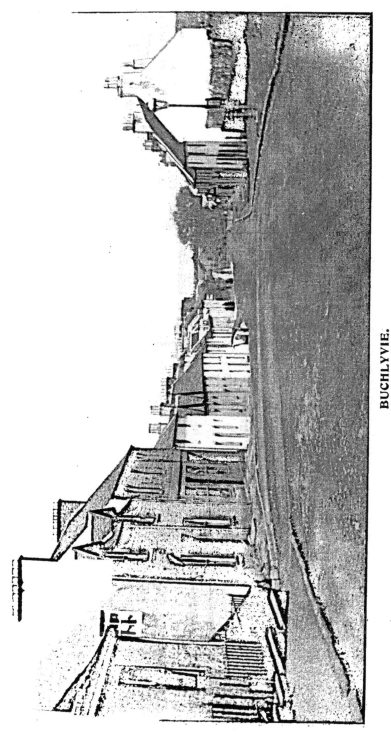

BUCHLYVIE.

relic of it remains, except a field called the "Castle Park." The "king of Kippen" was the second son of the brave Auchmar, Chief of the Buchanans. On one occasion he intercepted the King's carrier on his way from the Royal forest on the banks of Loch Lomond to Stirling Castle, and helped himself to some venison, remarking at the same time, that "Although your master be King of Scotland, I am 'king of Kippen.'" The King (James V.) shortly afterwards paid a visit to Arnprior, introducing himself as the "Guidman o' Ballangeich," and was sumptuously entertained.

Captain Cunningham of Boquhan (east of Kippen), one of the best swordsmen of his time, meeting Rob Roy at Arnprior, they had a sword bout. Cunningham had a bad squint, which discomfited the Macgregor and made him yield, convinced at the first onset that he was no match for the renowned swordsman. The old thatched corner house is still occupied where Rob Roy and Captain Cunningham frequently foregathered over a "reeking bowl."

A short distance east is the farm of Arnbeg, on the lands of which is a spot known as the *Preacher's Howe*, where, in 1675, according to Woodrow, the historian of the Covenanters, the Lord's Supper was dispensed under cloud of night to a great assembly.

Leaving Buchlyvie by the West.

Returning to Buchlyvie, and leaving by the west, fully a mile from the village, is *Ballochneck*, at one time the property of the author of "Lennie's

Grammar," well-known to former generations of the schoolboys of Scotland. Mr Lennie was the first to introduce bone manuring into the district, and it is said some of the farmers wives refused to use turnips grown upon ground where the manure was scattered, as they were, not unwarrantably, afraid of a mixture of human bones. The present proprietor is Mr. Wm. M'Onie, grandson of Sir Wm. M'Onie, late Lord Provost of Glasgow.

Following this road, 1½ miles from Buchlyvie, the visitor should turn down by the side of Ballochneck Burn, between the farms of Lower Ballaird and Craighead, for about 100 yards, and view the "*Muckle Spoot.*" This waterfall, 40 feet high and 20 feet wide, presents an interesting sight, and more particularly in winter, when that unseen architect and builder, "John Frost," has been at work, forming large pendent masses and grotesquely-shaped figures, transforming the scene into a veritable fairyland.

From the trough stone near here, or, better still, the higher ground of Gowston or Ballaird Farm, the prespect is extensive and varied. Immediately around and below is beautifully undulating ground, diversified with smiling fields and thriving plantations, and stretching along the valley of the Forth towards Stirling, in striking contrast, is that great flat, *Flanders Moss*, with the romantic Lake of Menteith at its edge, sparkling like a diamond, and sheltered on the north by the beautiful Menteith Hills, behind which, amid the magnificent display of mountain peaks, is the massive Ben Ledi, due north; and beyond, a little to the east, Ben Voirlich rises from Glenartney's braes;

ADVERTISEMENTS.

WM. STEELE

(Successor to R. M'QUISTON),

Family Butcher,
BUCHLYVIE.

**BEST HOME-FED BEEF AND MUTTON
AT MODERATE CHARGES.**

Vans call as follows:—

DRYMEN, BALMAHA, and CROFTAMIE,
  MONDAY and FRIDAY.

ABERFOYLE,
  TUESDAY and SATURDAY.

BALFRON,
  MONDAY, THURSDAY, and SATURDAY.

GARTMORE,
  WEDNESDAY and FRIDAY.

☞ *ORDERS STRICTLY ATTENDED TO.*

ADVERTISEMENTS.

WM. RICHARDSON,

Family Baker, Cook and Confectioner,
BUCHLYVIE.

Awarded Third Prize, Class C, for Loaf Bread at the Confectioners', Bakers', and Kindred Trades' Fifth Annual International Exhibition, Royal Agricultural Hall, London.

BRIDE CAKES,
BIRTHDAY CAKES,
AND
CHRISTENING CAKES.

INFANTS' OR INVALID RUSKS.
DISHES COVERED.

TEA ROOM.   **Parties purveyed for.**

All Orders to be delivered receive prompt attention and are carefully packed and despatched as desired.

in a north-westerly direction, Ben Venue and Ben A'n guard the fairy scene of the Trossachs; and in the same direction, the lofty peaks of Ben More and Stobinnain rise side by side above the Braes of Balquhidder, while in the west is the well-defined and unmistakable summit of Ben Lomond.

A little further along, on the farm of Mill of Cashly, there is a fort or camp called *The Keir* (a corruption of caer, a fort or camp), apparently in an excellent state of preservation.

Another mound, and what seems also to have been a camp, immediately comes into view in a field on Balwill Farm. It is 120 yards in circumference, and is known as the *Beech Knowe*, or *Lady Stirling's Knoll*. Overgrown with fine beech trees of uncertain age, this mound has a striking and picturesque appearance.

Before reaching Lower Ballaird Farm, taking Balwill Road to the right, and crossing the Forth and Clyde Railway, the entrance to *Auchentroig* will be found on the left, after passing on the right the road leading to Buchlyvie Station. For 600 years the M'Lachlans resided in this house. The last of this family, Mr. Wm. A. M'Lachlan, died in October, 1884. In 1710 Rob Roy and his men "lifted" all the sheep and cattle on the estate, and besieged the house to capture the laird as security for future blackmail. It was only after fire was applied to the massive oaken door that the defence ended, and the laird was carried to Aberfoyle. After the payment of the usual ransom he was released. The old door still swings in its place, with the marks of the flames still visible. The present proprietor is Mr. Euing R. Crawford.

Kippen.

KIPPEN is an attractive, old country village, occupying a commanding position, with indications in its modern cottages and villas of growing prosperity and popularity as a summer resort. It is 9½ miles west of Stirling, and about one mile from the station on the Forth and Clyde Railway. The population of the parish in 1901 was 1450, and of the village 350. The parish of Kippen is partly in Perthshire and partly in Stirlingshire, and includes, in addition to the village of Kippen, the village of Buchlyvie and the hamlets of Shirgarton, Cauldhame, Arnprior, and Kepp.

Pursuits.

The majority of the villagers are dependent on agriculture. *The Forth Vineries*, to the west of the village, are most extensive, and the scene they present in summer will amply repay a visit from the tourist. The parish at one time was the seat of whisky distillation. North of the boundary line between the Highlands and the Lowlands an old Act of Parliament permitted a somewhat free manufacture of whisky, and the good folks of Kippen who claimed to be on the privileged side, took full advantage of this freedom till a new Act was passed in 1793.

Some Interesting Features.

There are two churches—the *Parish Church* and the *United Free Church*. The former is a solid, substantial building of red sandstone. In its square tower a handsome clock finds fit habitation. The windows of the church are mostly of stained-glass, and of a memorial character. The United Free Church is a light and graceful structure. It is the second church occupied by this congregation since the Disruption, and its erection was largely owing to the munificence and energy of the late minister, Rev. Mr. Muirhead, whose memory is suitably perpetuated on the walls within, by a marble tablet.

In the *Old Churchyard*, surrounding the ivied relic of a former Parish Church, slumber men whose very existence was a struggle, and whose life was one long heroic battle in the cause of freedom. The inhabitants of the Parish of Kippen were zealous Covenanters. At the battle of Bothwell Bridge, a body of 200 or 300 men, made up partly with Covenanters from Kippen, was placed as a guard upon the bridge, and defended it with great gallantry. Conspicuous was Ure of Shirgarton, a stern and devoted Covenanter, who suffered much persecution at the hands of the Stuarts. His body reposes here. The family of Edenbellie also find a resting-place here. It was for robbing this family of their daughter, Jean Kay, that young Rob Roy forfeited his life on the scaffold at Edinburgh, 16th February, 1754.

The village contains the *Gillespie Memorial Hall*,

a splendid tribute to the zeal and energy of the late Rev. William Wilson, a former parish minister. Part of the furnishings of the hall is a valuable and well selected library, available to villagers and visitors at a small subscription.

There is another hall in the village, known as the *Public Hall*, which, within a couple of years ago, was the Old Parish or Public School. So abounding are the spirit and activity of the people of the village and vicinity that in winter both halls are in full and constant use.

Kippen has the distinction of being the only parish in the district that has a *Cemetery*. It is pleasantly situated near the junction of the roads leading to the village and to Stirling, three-quarters of a mile from the village, and $4\frac{1}{4}$ from Buchlyvie. It may be noted that access is only to be had occasionally. The key is three miles off, and, as the writer knows from experience, the iron paling is a rather formidable one to negotiate.

At the *Fords of Frew*, hardly a quarter-mile north of Kippen Station, on the Doune Road, the Pretender's Army crossed the Forth in safety on their way to Falkirk. At this place there is now a bridge, by no means complimentary to the County Council, but likely to stand until, like its predecessor, it collapses.

Boquhan House is a mile to the east of the village. Here the ill-fated Prince Charles dined on his retreat northwards.

Boquhan Glen is one of the grandest in the county of Stirling, and scarcely inferior to the famous Trossachs. On the banks of the Glen is the old battle

KIPPEN.

CROSS KEYS HOTEL,

MAIN STREET, KIPPEN.

Fully a Mile from Station on the Forth and Clyde line.

ACCOMMODATION FOR TRAVELLERS, TOURISTS, AND FAMILIES.

VISITORS to "The Kingdom" will find this a comfortable Hotel, and Charges Moderate.

LUNCHEONS. DINNERS. TEAS.

QUARTERS OF SCOTTISH CYCLISTS' UNION.

R. BUCHANAN,
Proprietor.

Natural Autumn=Tinted Vine Leaves.

Testimonial from HER LATE MAJESTY THE QUEEN.

"Sir Henry Ponsonby begs to inform Messrs. D. & W. Buchanan that the Autumn-Tinted Vine Leaves which they forwarded on the 7th inst. were duly given to the Queen, and Her Majesty has commanded that her thanks should be returned to Messrs. D. & W. Buchanan for same.

"Privy Purse Office, Buckingham Palace, S.W."

VINE LEAVES supplied from first week in October to middle of December only. Leaves 1s. 9d. per box, post free; MAIDEN-HAIR FERN FRONDS, 1s. 1d. per box, post free.

SPECIAL ASSORTMENT to make up arrangement in Vase or Epergne, 2 boxes Vine Leaves, 6 long Fronds, "Lomaria Spicant," 6 large beautiful green Fern-like leaves of "Grevillea Robusta," 6 large Fronds Maiden-Hair Fern. All preserved to keep fresh without water, by new process, with wires, and full directions how to make up, in each parcel. Carriage Free to any part of the United Kingdom for 5/6.

The above makes one of the most lovely and unique decorations that it is possible to conceive.

Highest Awards at every important Horticultural Exhibition in Britain.
☞ DIPLOMA OF HONOUR, Glasgow International Exhibition, 1901.

GRAPES and **TOMATOES** a Speciality.

D. & W. BUCHANAN, Forth Vineyards, KIPPEN, N.B.

ground of *Balloch Chlean,* the scene of a terrible conflict between the Grahams of Dundaff and the Leckies of Leckie. On the other side of the Glen, and rising out of the bed of a feeder of the Boquhan Burn, there is a natural tower of some interest, as it was the hiding-place in persecuting times of a local Covenanter, whose name it perpetuates, under the designation of "Dougal" Tower.

Natural Features and Prospects.

The *Muir of Kippen* extends in the direction of Balgair, in the parish of Balfron. Red sandstone is plentiful here, and is quarried for building purposes; while limestone is to be found on the southern border, but owing to the absence of coal in the neighbourhood, has been little wrought. Along the northern boundary the Forth winds its way within a narrow channel, and presents a rather sluggish appearance.

From a half to three-quarters of a mile to the south of the Forth, the ground rises sharply by a series of natural terraces to the *Wright Park* and *Kippen Moors,* and then, with the exception of a deep and sudden descent to the south of the Wright Park Moor, caused by the Boquhan Glen, it rises sheer to the summit of the Gargunnock and Fintry Hills. From almost any point in the course of this ascent views hardly to be equalled for impressiveness and extent may be had on a clear day. The nearer of the Grampians appear to lie at our feet as we look to the north over the Vale of Menteith and Flanders Moss, as if they had, like a mighty tide, been suddenly arrested in their southward flow, and thrown into huge peaks of spray—Ben Venue, Ben Ledi, Ben Voirlich, and Uam Var in the nearer prospect; Ben Cruachan, Ben Lui, Ben More, Stobinnain, in the remoter one; to the east we may see past Abbey Craig to the Hills of Benarty and the Lomonds in Fifeshire; to the west Ben Lomond, with his broad shoulder, jealous of his reputation, blocks the view of his giant rival in Arran.

In full view of such a panorama lies the first three miles of the road from Kippen to Fintry, Balfron, and Killearn, by way of Kippen Muir; and, in the descent on the other side, the view of the lovely valley of the Endrick, less extensive, is equally impressive, and probably more enchanting.

Places of Interest.

Distance from Village.

Aberfoyle,	13 miles.
Loch Ard,	14 miles.
Trossachs,	18 miles.
Lake of Menteith,	8 miles.
Callander,	10 miles.
Doune,	8 miles.
Dunblane,	11 miles.
Blair Drummond,	6 miles.
Stirling,	$9\frac{1}{2}$ miles.
Fords of Frew,	$1\frac{1}{4}$ miles.
Fintry,	6 miles.

GUIDE
TO
THE LAKE OF MENTEITH.

THE *Lake of Menteith* is about equally distant (between 3 and 4 miles) from three railway stations, Port of Menteith, Aberfoyle, and Gartmore.

From Port of Menteith Station to the Lake.

The walk from Port of Menteith Station is exceedingly pleasant. On the right, amid grand old trees, is *Cardross House*, the seat of Mr. H. D. Erskine, a representative of an old and noble family.

Half-way between the Station and the Lake is a grassy knoll upon the left side of the road called *Tamavhoid*, which tradition records was the Tyburn of the Port in the days when summary, or Jeddart, justice was dispensed by the lord of the manor. The Port must have been desperately wicked in days past, as on the northern side of the lake, facing the "gallus" hill of Tamavhoid, is another such hill, which until recently bore upon its crest the reputed gibbet tree. Half-a-mile further on the Old Mill Brae is reached, and of the nature of its declivity cyclists are warned by the legend, near Lochend Farm, "This hill is dangerous." Then we come to the *Goodie Burn*. This being the only outlet from the lake, there is usually a considerable flow of water, and trout fishers have had good "takes" from this stream. After passing Inchie Farm, there is near the lake an eminence, where, in the palmy days of the Priory of Inchmahome, was a chapel in which service was held when the lake was too stormy for the parishioners to cross to the island.

The Port.

Two and a half miles from the station, the southeast corner of the Lake being reached, the road skirts the Lake for about another mile ere the traveller arrives at the Port, which includes the Church and the Hotel.

The *Church*, erected in 1878, is a neat edifice in the Gothic style, and distinguished from all other churches in the district by having a chime of bells. In the churchyard are to be found the last resting-places of the Grahams.

The Lake.

The *Lake* has a circumference of 6 or 7 miles, its dimensions from east to west being about a mile and a half, and from north to south about one mile. The visitor will be impressed by its peaceful appearance, the rugged surroundings so characteristic of Scottish Lochs being absent. The placid waters, wooded banks, and soft pastoral beauty, make this region a fit resting-place amid the tension of life and toil. Nature here speaks more audibly than the most impassioned eloquence from human lips. Amid such scenes the distracting cares and empty joys of the world are all forgotten; and there is within gratitude, devotion, and the hope that looks beyond.

The Islands.

There are three islands, Inchmahome, Inchtalla, and Inchcuan, the first two being richly wooded, lending additional beauty to the Lake.

Inchmahome.

Inchmahome ("The Isle of Rest"), the largest island, is about 6 acres in extent. There is much about it of historical and antiquarian interest, containing as it does the remains of an extensive and noted Priory, the ruins leaving no doubt as to its original grandeur and importance, and being the whilom residence in her childhood of Mary Queen of Scots.

During the season, "The Macgregor," a trim little steam launch, accommodating about 40 passengers, and the property of Mr. Macgregor, the enterprising lessee of the hotel, plies upon the Lake for the benefit of tourists and excursionists. It touches at the island of Inchmahome, where the "voyagers" may land and meditate among the mouldering cloisters, fallen columns, and Gothic arches of pre-Reformation times; repose beneath the shade of the venerable Spanish chestnut trees, whose antlered limbs and indented trunks have weathered the blasts of centuries; or, wandering among the overgrown box-wood, the ear may catch "booming down to us through the dark corridors of time," the pattering of the little feet or the merry voices of Scotland's unhappy Queen and her Maries.

The Priory.

The *Priory*, standing on slightly rising ground on the north side of the island, belonged to the canons regular of the Augustinian Order, and was founded by King Edgar in 1106. Originally it was connected with the Abbey of Cambuskenneth, afterwards attached by James IV. to the Royal Chapel of Stirling, and eventually bestowed by James V. upon John, Lord Erskine, as commendatory abbot. It was visited by King Robert the Bruce in 1310, and also by James VI.

The buildings include a Church, with the usual

accessories, and also accommodation for the Prior and Canons of the monastic establishment. In the west wall is the main doorway of the Church. This doorway, as may be seen from our illustration, is a splendid example of early English Gothic architecture.

Queen Mary's Residence.

When the English invaded Scotland in 1547, with the view of compelling a marriage contract between Edward VI. and Mary, then five years of age, she was taken to the Priory for safety.

A romantic interest attaches to the island as the brief abode of the child Queen. There is little doubt that in this secluded spot, the beautiful and unfortunate Mary Queen of Scots spent the happiest days of her eventful life. Memorials of her residence are to be found in *Queen Mary's Chamber*, over the Chapter House; *Queen Mary's Garden*, an enclosure about 30 yards square in the south-west part of the island, and surrounded by an old stone wall, and, in the centre of the garden, *Queen Mary's Tree*, a boxtree about 20 feet high, said to have been planted by her hand; while to the west of this enclosure, on a mound sloping towards the Lake, is an oval plot known as *Queen Mary's Bower*, in the centre of which is an old thorn tree, and round about a narrow box-bordered path.

Before leaving this interesting island the visitor, matrimonially inclined, should not omit trying to throw a particular stone over the certain branch of a

PRIORY OF INCHMAHOME.

given tree. If this feat be successfully performed, a happy marriage is assured within the year.

Inchtalla (Celtic "a hall"), to the west of Inchmahome, contain the ruins of the ancient home of the Earls of Menteith.

Inchcuan ("the Isle of Dogs"), the third and smallest island, is near the western shore. This is where the Earls had their dog-kennel, and the dogs kept by them were of some repute, as His Majesty, James VI., wrote in August, 1617, to the Earl of Mar for "Two couple of excellent terrieres or earth dogges, which are both stoute and good fox killers, and will stay long in the ground," and he understands that the "Earl of Menteith hath good of that kinde who wee are sure wilbe glade to gratifie us with them."

Angling.

Excellent sport may be got on the Lake fishing for pike or perch. Trolling from a boat is the usual method adopted. Various kinds of bait are used, such as fresh or preserved minnows, gudgeon or garvies or eeltail, or small trout for natural bait, while artificial minnow of various colours and sizes to suit the season and condition of water and light are just as good.

There are some trout which have escaped the ravages of the pike, and therefore of good size. It is to be regretted that nothing has been done to make this a trouting lake. The pike need not be exterminated, as it is said that where this has been done the trout, by overstocking, have become lean and ill-conditioned. Were this lake attended to, it would be easier of access than Loch Leven for the fishing fraternity from the west of Scotland.

On the placid surface of the Lake is to be found the white water lily (Nymphaea alba). Its broad, glossy, heart-shaped leaves and snow-white blossoms are singularly beautiful and attractive, and lovers of our flora, if they wish to see

"The water lily to the light
Her chalice rear of silver bright,"

should explore the sedgy shores and bays.

The yellow water lily (Nymphaea lutea), water grasses, and other aquatic plants, including the great bulrush (Scirpus palustris), are to be found in the lake.

Walks and Prospects.

There are several delightful walks in which the visitor may indulge, none daring to make him afraid.

The loftiest height in the parish is *Ben Dearig* (1401 feet), situated due north from the Port Hotel, and all lovers of mountaineering must accomplish this ascent while in the Port. The young and venturesome, who always take the short cut, attack the hill just behind the school, but ere they reach the summit of the Port Craig a few breathing spaces have to be indulged in. However, when this ascent is made, the arduous part of the climb is over, and, after crossing a gentle slope, in half-an-hour the summit of the Ben is reached. If the day be clear a wide range of vision is obtained. The whole Vale of Menteith is unrolled before the eye of the spectator, stretching from beyond Gartmore on the west, to the Ochils and the Firth of Forth on the east, while behind, to the north, the Grampians rise ridge upon ridge, whose nearer crests we recognise in Ben Ledi, Ben Voirlich, Ben Venue, and Ben A'n. From here can be traced the course followed by the stag in that famous chase in the "Lady of the Lake," from just behind Callander, where

> The stag at eve had drunk his fill
> Where danced the moon on Monan's rill,
> And deep his midnight lair had made
> In lone Glenartney's hazel shade."

to where the stag

> "Dashing down a darksome glen,
> Soon lost to hound and hunter's ken,
> In the deep Trossachs' wildest nook
> His solitary refuge took."

The easier, though more circuitous, ascent is by Glenny Farm, from which a due east course leads to the summit. Ben Dearig means the red hill. There are several of this name in the Highlands, named probably from the red moss found on the mountains.

Another delightful walk is by Glenny Farm, through the Scheeper's Pass, to the southern shore of Loch Vennacher. There is not much climbing to be done, and the walk can be accomplished (both going and returning) between breakfast and dinner.

From the Port Toll, eastwards on the Stirling road,

the path is beautifully shaded with trees as far as Blairhoyle (2 miles east), the property of Mr. George Crabbie. One mile east is Hammersmith, at which place the road branches to the left to Callander, while the other holds on to Thornhill and Stirling. One mile beyond Hammersmith, on the Callander road, to the right, is Loch Ruskie, on the shores of which the "fause John Menteith" had his abode.

Another excellent walk is westward from the Port Toll, four miles, to Aberfoyle. A very pretty view is obtained from the top of Malling Brae, in which the islands of the lake and the peninsula of Arnmauck are clearly defined.

The telegraph was introduced into the Port two years ago, and it is expected that a branch railway will soon be brought into the Port, either from Gartmore Station, or better still, from Doune (10 miles from Port), with a station at the village of Thornhill, and another at the hamlet of Ruskie, terminating in the Port. The latter would not overlap any other company's line, which, unfortunately, formed the principal objection to the Port of Menteith Railway Bill some years ago. Such a railway from Doune would be welcomed by the parishioners and farmers along the valley of Menteith, and would open up to the visitor one of the loveliest vales in Scotland.

Gartmore.

THE village of Gartmore, nestling amidst scenery of utmost grandeur, occupies a commanding situation in the south-west corner of Perthshire. It is possible here, planting one foot in Stirlingshire and the other in Perthshire, to wash your face in the burn that divides the counties. The fine position of this village is due to the frugal character of its founder. The Laird of Gartmore of that day proposed letting feus for building purposes in the plain below, but as this was fertile ground, on the principle of economy the rocky eminence on which the village stands was chosen. The history of Gartmore dates for a period of 300 years, and it was once a most important centre when one of the few roads from the Highlands passed through it. The old residenters say that the village in their youthful days was the admiration of all strangers, with its single street, lined on either side by fine old trees, spreading their branches over the clean white-washed houses. In front there is a fine panorama of beauty—hill and dale, wood and water stretching away beyond Stirling town and Castle until the view is lost in the dim distance. There are two churches, an Established and United Free, the Rev. Malcolm M'Lean having ministered to the latter for a period of 38 years. The village has a fine Circulating Library, the gift of the firm of J. & A. M'Donald, well-known Glasgow merchants, and natives of the district.

Gartmore House, which has undergone considerable alterations by the present proprietor, Sir Charles Cayzer, M.P., is built on an eminence a little to the east of the village. It was the seat for many generations, till 1900, of the ancient and honourable family of Graham, the last proprietor of the name being the well-known and brilliant R. B. Cunninghame-Graham, who sold the estate to the present proprietor. The first Graham of Gartmore appears to have been Robert, second son of John, fourth Earl of Menteith. A name held dear by the Gartmore people is that of Robert Graham, born in 1730. He was M.P. for the county of Stirling, Lord Rector of Glasgow University, and founder of Gartmore Gold Medal competed for by students every second year. Burns wrote of him—"He is the noblest instance of great talents, great fortune, and great worth that I ever saw in conjunction." Sir Walter Scott paid a long visit to Gartmore House, and "Rob Roy" was mainly plotted and written there.

About a mile north-west of the village is *Blairnabord*, which derives its name from being the residence of the bards of the early lairds of Gartmore.

A mile and a half west from the village, in a rather inaccessible region, there is a remarkable seam of porphyry, admired for its beauty by the late Professor Henry Drummond. This quarry is on the lands of the Duke of Montrose, and was for a number of years wrought by a Glasgow Company. The stone, being ground, was utilised in the manufacture (or adulteration) of paint. The difficulty and expense of working the seam were such that all operations have ceased.

ADVERTISEMENTS.

BEST HOUSE COAL

BY WAGGON OR CART,

DELIVERED AT RESIDENCE OF PURCHASER.

Arrangements have been made, on receiving notice, to convey LUGGAGE of all descriptions from or to the Station.

M. FERGUSON,
GARTMORE STATION.

D. H. HALDANE,

General Merchant and News Agent,

GARTMORE.

ORDERS FOR GOODS NOT IN STOCK PUNCTUALLY ATTENDED TO.

MORNING, EVENING, and WEEKLY PAPERS, and PERIODICALS.

LOCAL VIEWS.

ADVERTISEMENTS.

BLACK BULL HOTEL, GARTMORE.

COMMERCIAL AND EXCURSIONISTS' HOTEL.

PURE, DRY, BRACING AIR.

WITHIN AN EASY WALKING OR DRIVING DISTANCE OF SOME OF THE GRANDEST SCENERY IN SCOTLAND.

PARTIES CATERED FOR.

POSTING.

JAMES KEIR, Proprietor.

Immediately to the south of the village was the "*Tapaltae*" of the district. These were round mounds called in English "Law," but corrupted into "Tapaltae," which means the top of the law where the civil and criminal affairs of the barony were executed.

A mile south of the village, where the road crosses the Kelty, is *Chapellarach*, a name at once suggesting a religious house. There was at one time a chapel here, the ruins of which were visible till the end of the eighteenth century, although nothing but the foundations are now to be seen. A farmhouse is now built on the spot. A public-house at this place was the scene of some lively events. In 1716 Rob Roy, after his own peculiar fashion, relieved Mr. Graham of Killearn, factor to the Duke of Montrose, of some rents which he had taken two days to collect. It was also here that his sons met, 34 years afterwards, to mature their plans for the abduction of Jean Kay, the heiress of Edenbellie; which proved an unfortunate episode in the history of the Macgregors.

The Claggan Glen, entered from the south part of the village, is a romantic place which was the scene of a supposed tragedy. A young man went to see his sweetheart one evening at a neighbouring farm, and as he did not return a search was made, with the result that his body was found in the glen at the foot of a steep rock, where it was supposed he had been thrown by a rival, who was known to be in the vicinity at the time. The writer, while on a fern hunting expedition, spent a few of the most exciting moments of his life here. He climbed the face of a rock to secure a fine specimen of

Hart's Tongue (Scolopendrium vulgare). It was only when about to retrace his steps that the perilous nature of his position dawned upon him. Cold sweat dropped from his brow, as he thought of being dashed to the foot. In some providential manner, however, he managed to scramble down in safety. That fern, for at least a dozen years, was tended with none the less care on account of the hazardous circumstances under which it was possessed.

About a mile and a half south of the Claggan, on the north-west bank of the Ward Burn, is an ancient and interesting stronghold called the *Peel of Gartfarran* (castle of vexation). This fort is in a good state of preservation, and is supposed to have been erected by the Romans to afford them protection from the assaults of the natives who inhabited the surrounding country. These military works are nearly square, and measure within the trenches about 50 paces either way. There are two ramparts and a ditch, both quite discernible. The circumference of the work measures 320 paces.

It is an interesting fact not generally known that the first victory achieved by General Wolfe (who fell at Quebec five years later) was in the immediate neighbourhood of Gartmore. When a subaltern Wolfe had active command of the Inversnaid garrison, and is said to have been the officer who led the picquet that captured young Rob Roy at a place called Balloch Roy, or the Red Pass, when on his way to the Fair of Gartmore. The late Professor M'Gregor, of New College, Edinburgh, contended that it was in the Claggan Glen where the capture took place.

ADVERTISEMENTS.

ESTABLISHED 52 YEARS.

GEORGE PATRICK,

Boot and Shoe Maker,

GARTMORE.

BOOTS and SHOES Made to Order or Fitted from Stock.

MATERIAL AND WORKMANSHIP GUARANTEED.

REPAIRS NEATLY EXECUTED.

MUNRO & JAMIESON,

PRINTERS, PUBLISHERS, and WHOLESALE STATIONERS,

26-32 Craigs, Stirling.

PUBLISHERS OF ✣ ✣

Stirling Saturday Observer.

Every Friday Evening.   One Penny.

Contains all the Local and District News of the Week.

An Excellent Family Paper.

Callander Advertiser.

Every Friday Evening.   One Penny.

Guide to Aberfoyle.

"The noble stag was pausing now
Upon the mountain's southern brow,
Where broad extended, far beneath,
The varied realms of fair Menteith.
With anxious eye he wandered o'er
Mountain and meadow, moss and moor,
And pondered refuse from his toil
By far Loch Ard or Aberfoyle."

THE Clachan of Aberfoyle and neighbourhood have undergone a great transformation since the days of Rob Roy, and that earliest recorded and most memorable excursion thereto of a Glasgow Bailie. The natural features of the district, as well as the life and characteristics of the rude inhabitants in that stirring time have been so deftly and happily portrayed by Sir Walter Scott in his great novel, that any extended endeavour to emulate him could only be described in such classic phrases as "ploughing the sands," or "whitewashing the rainbow;" while to quote him at length would be wearisome to writer and reader alike.

Both are, however, unavoidable if we are to traverse

BAILIE NICOL JARVIE HOTEL, ABERFOYLE.

and explore this beautiful and romantic country, which the great magician, it may almost be said, created for us with the wave of his grey-goose wand, and the visitor who does so with this book for his guide should adopt "Rob Roy" as philosopher and friend.

The Clachan Inn.

Mistress Jean Macalpine's Inn, where she greeted Francis Osbaldistone, Andrew Fairservice, and Bailie Nicol Jarvie with "a lighted piece of split fir blazing in her hand, has succumbed to the inevitable. Curiously enough, the "Bailie Nicol Jarvie" now opens wide his hospitable door to the wayfarer, but not to reveal an interior which "presented a view which seemed singular enough to Southern eyes. The fire, fed with blazing turf and branches of dried wood, blazed merrily in the centre; but the smoke, having no means to escape but through a hole in the roof, eddied round the rafters of the cottage, and hung in sable folds at the height of about five feet from the floor. The space beneath was kept pretty clear by innumerable currents of air which rushed towards the fire from the broken panel of basket-work which served as a door—from the two square holes, designed as ostensible windows, through one of which was thrust a plaid and through the other a tattered greatcoat. . . . Cribs (beds) there were of different dimensions beside the walls, formed, some of fractured boards, some of shattered wicker-work or plaited boughs, in which slumbered the family of the house, men, women, and children, their places of repose only concealed by the dusky wreaths of vapour which arose above, below, and around them."

Such is the picture of this hospitable dwelling, and of the domestic felicity shared by a party, including a Magistrate of dignity and standing, fresh from the luxury and culture of his own beloved Sautmarket, only 28 miles away. And the stable—"Where horses were stowed away along with goats, poultry, pigs, and cows, under the same roof with the mansion-house," must have been very convenient indeed.

The Ancient Clachan.

The miserable little "bourocks," of which about a dozen formed the village called the *Clachan of Aberfoyle*, were composed of loose stones cemented by clay instead of mortar, and thatched by turfs laid rudely upon rafters formed of native and unhewn birches and oaks from the woods around. The roofs approached the ground so nearly that Andrew Fairservice observed—"We might have ridden over the village the night before and never found out we were near it, unless our horses' feet had gone through the riggin'."

The Modern Clachan.

Needless to say, the social, sanitary, and architectural conditions of this interesting clachan have altered greatly since the "Wizard" peopled it with those lively creatures of his fancy, who have survived their own times to delight ours.

It is now, in the season, quite a gay place, with a

convenient railway station, well equipped shops, comfortable villas, ornamental cottages, exhibiting tasteful freaks of architecture, and in addition to the Parish Church an Episcopalian.

Natural Features.

Nature, however, even human nature, changes not, and so we may be content to leave unregretted the smoky squalor of the "bourocks," and the rude life of their inmates, to view the fair landscape which still remains "land of brown heath and shaggy wood," while mountain, loch, and river, reckless of the changing years or ebbing centuries, combine, as in days of yore, to rejoice the eye and seduce the senses. The beholder to-day looks upon, as did Sir Walter Scott, a land of beauty and romance, enhanced by the magic of the spell he cast about it. Sir Walter wrote:—"Such a scene of natural romance and beauty had never before greeted my eyes. To the left lay the valley, down which the Forth wandered on its easterly course, surrounding the beautiful detached hill, with all its garland of woods. On the right, amid a profusion of thickets, knolls, and crags lay the bed of a broad mountain lake, lightly curled into tiny waves by the breath of the morning breeze, each glittering in its course under the influence of the sunbeams. High hills, rocks, and banks, waving with natural forests of birch and oak, formed the borders of this enchanting sheet of water; and as their leaves rustled to the wind, and twinkled in the sun, gave to the depth of solitude a sort of life and vivacity. Man alone seemed to be placed in a state of inferiority in a scene where all the ordinary features of nature were raised and exalted."

The Coulter.

On a chain, from the limb of an oak tree of peculiar form in front of the hotel, hangs the identical *coulter* handled with such unexpected and telling effect by Bailie Nicol Jarvie against his great, sturdy, hairy-legged, kilted antagonist, Alister Mactavish. The coulter still blushes to find itself famous, and the remarkable fact has been observed that the blush appears to be periodically revived or renewed. The combat in the inn is perhaps the most amusing scene in "Rob Roy."

"The Long Low Bridge."

Opposite the hotel is "*the long low bridge*" over the Forth, so graphically described in "Rob Roy." It was upon this bridge that Graham of Duchray, aided and abetted by the minister of Aberfoyle, who had just baptized a child of Graham's in the old Church close by, met and repulsed the "beagles" who had come from Stirling to arrest him for debt. Surrounded by his retainers, he defied the minions of the law to come further, threatening, if they did so, to drown the one half and kill the other. Fortunately for themselves, the party considered discretion the better part of valour, and prudently retired.

The Old Church and Churchyard.

About a quarter of a mile further south, is the *Old*

OLD ABERFOYLE.

Church and *Churchyard*. One of the most interesting tombstones in the churchyard is that erected to the memory of the Rev. Robert Kirk, A.M., who died in the year 1692, and notable as the author of a curious essay on the nature and actions of the Fairies. According to tradition, the touchy little people were so indignant at the publication of their secrets, that they carried him off to the Fairy Knowe, where he still remains a prisoner.

On either side of the door of the old Church can still be seen two iron mort safes, which were used to enclose or cover newly interred coffins at the period, not so very remote, when Aberfoyle churchyard shared the attentions of those hated ghouls, the "resurrectionists," or body-snatchers.

The Manse of Aberfoyle, near the old Church, is of interest, being the house in which Sir Walter Scott was a guest during his visit to the neighbourhood. It is said that many of the stories and legends from which he wove the romantic tale of "Rob Roy," were related to him by the Rev. Patrick Graham, the genial and accomplished minister of the parish at the time.

The Golf Course.

About a mile eastward from the station lies the *Golf Course*. It is one of nine holes, and will bear comparison with any inland course of similar size. The turf being very old hill pasture, and the soil of a sandy nature, the course may always be found in first-rate condition; while the scenery it commands embraces some of the finest in central Scotland. There is a neat and comfortable club-house.

The Churches.

A short distance west from the hotel is the new *Parish Church*. It was built in 1870 by the late Mr. Robert Hampson and Mrs. Richard Hampson, his sister-in-law, of the Glassert, in memory of the husband of the latter and the brother of the former. In the year 1884 it was enlarged and beautified by the same generous hands. This is one of the prettiest Parish Churches in Scotland, and is well worth a visit.

St. Mary's Episcopal Church, built 1894, is an exceedingly neat Gothic edifice, seated for 180, situated on a rising knoll at the east end of the Clachan, and two minutes walk from the station.

To Loch Ard, Loch Chon, and Stronachlachar.

Proceeding along this road towards *Loch Ard*, which can now be done without fear of the cateran or of the hostile clan, an immense debris of detached rock is observed. This, the accumulation of ages, has fallen from the overhanging cliffs of Craigmore, which rises almost perpendicularly to a height of 1271 feet. Legend has it that when a rock falls a Macgregor dies, not at all an unlikely story if the Macgregor were lodged underneath when the rock was dislodged.

At Craigmuick, a mile from the road, the *Duchray Water* forms the march line at this part between the counties of Stirling and Perth.

On either hand along this road one will find glimpses of beauty to please the eye and rejoice the

ADVERTISEMENTS.

WM. LOCKHART & SONS

(Successors to WM. FORREST),

Bakers, Purveyors, & Confectioners,

ABERFOYLE.

SHOP and TEA ROOMS opposite RAILWAY STATION.

WEDDING CAKES of Artistic Design.

CHRISTENING and BIRTHDAY CAKES.

FANCY BISCUITS of Superior Quality.

VISITORS TO ABERFOYLE
Will find TEA ROOMS Convenient and Comfortable, Articles of Best Quality, and Charges Moderate.

VANS DELIVER REGULARLY THROUGHOUT DISTRICT.

PARTIES AND EXCURSIONISTS CATERED FOR.

LARGE HALL in connection with Establishment.

Telegrams—"LOCKHART, ABERFOYLE."

ADVERTISEMENTS.

Bailie Nicol Jarvie Hotel,
ABERFOYLE.

EXCELLENT ACCOMMODATION FOR TOURISTS AND FAMILIES.

COACHES
To and from the TROSSACHS and LOCH KATRINE Daily.

The DRIVES
In the Neighbourhood in Scenes of "The Lady of the Lake" and romance of Sir Walter Scott, are unsurpassed in any part of the Scottish Highlands.

BOATS
On LOCH ARD and LOCH CHON.

BILLIARDS.   TENNIS LAWN.   GOLF.   POSTING.

RAILWAY STATION, POST and TELEGRAPH OFFICE, within Two Minutes' walk of Hotel.

A. BLAIR, *Proprietor.*

heart of the most fastidious lover or the most exacting critic of Nature, and which have furnished studies of loveliness at once the delight and despair of painters and poets innumerable.

A mile from Aberfoyle the first view of Loch Ard greets the eye. This lower part is of no great extent, and is connected with the upper loch by a narrow, shallow channel, barely navigable. Away to the west the peak of Ben Lomond pierces the sky, in the foreground numerous eminences clad in verdure to their summits with grey, rugged rocks, here and there peeping through, and below the narrow lower loch, presently expanding to a width of half-a-mile, and extending a mile; while on the right the lower half of the hillside is covered with woods, where flourish in wild profusion the rowan, the sloe, and the hazel.

This is the *Pass of Aberfoyle*, the barrier in the "good old times" between the lowlands and the wilder regions of the west, and the scene of many a fierce encounter in those days of feud and foray. Before the road was made a few daring warriors here could make sad havoc in the ranks of an enemy, as the troops of Cromwell experienced when their attempt to force the Pass was defeated by a band of Highlanders under the Earl of Glencairn and Graham of Duchray.

Here, in the Pass, and stretching into the Loch, is the great rock from which Helen Macgregor, sword in hand and pistols at her girdle, extended cousinly welcome to her canny kinsman and his friends from Glasgow.

Following the road for fully a mile, the water is lost sight of for a time, but it may be joined again where the path leads southward through the woods to the rocks overshadowing the connecting stream, where, perhaps, the finest view of the loch is to be had.

Directly westward, Ben Lomond closes the view, towering on the right is Bonoghrie, and below, Loch Ard lies in fairest prospect, the rocky islands near the southern shore ornament its surface, while its shores are beautified with wood and coppice, and at its northern and western extremities with meadows, cornfields, and farmhouses, looking the more lovely from their proximity to the predominating sternness around. Proceeding westward along the side of the loch, the visitor will notice a rocky precipice from 30 feet to 50 feet high. Under this rock a very distinct echo is returned from the other side of the loch.

Rob Roy's Cave, on the south shore, is capable of holding forty men within its rocky walls. Some years ago a gentleman in the district had a coloured gamekeeper. For his own amusement and his friends' "entertainment," a favourite scheme was a visit to the cave. Before leaving the house, however, he invariably gave his sable henchman the hint as to what was on foot, and he proceeded in front, and secreted himself in the cave. On the company arriving at the cave, the gentleman called out—"Are you in, Rob?" when a black head popped out, greatly to the alarm and discomfiture of the company.

Duke Murdoch's Island is a small wooded island near the south shore. Murdoch, Duke of Albany, Regent of Scotland during the captivity of James I. in England, constructed a fortress here in view of the danger to his person in the event of his cousin, James

I., returning to Scotland and ascending the throne. He is said to have been taken from his castle on this isolated rock to Stirling for trial and execution. Only two months elapsed from the time of his arrest till he was beheaded at Stirling Castle.

Near the head of the loch is *St. Malloch*, an island containing the remains of an old chapel said to be dedicated to its patron saint.

The Fall of Ledard is a short distance above the farmhouse of Ledard, and opposite the head of the loch. The water falls in one sheet from a height of 12 feet into a circular basin, locally named Flora Macdonald's Shower Bath, from which it dashes over a peculiarly formed ledge of rock, and precipitates itself again over an irregular slope of over 60 feet. Growing on either side of this slope, out of crevices of the rock, are many old and curiously formed trees. This fall has been made classic by Scott in "Rob Roy" and "Waverley."

Two miles beyond Loch Ard, *Loch Chon* opens up. It is a fine sheet of water about $2\frac{1}{2}$ miles long by half-a-mile broad.

From the foot of Loch Chon to *Loch Arklet* is about 4 miles, and a mile further on, turning to the right, *Stronachlachar*, on the banks of Loch Katrine, is reached.

From Aberfoyle to the Trossachs.

From Aberfoyle Hotel to the Trossachs Hotel, on the north shore of Loch Achray, the distance is six miles, and four-in-hand coaches make this journey several times a day during the season. A short distance north of the hotel, on the right, there is a magnificent waterfall. The small mountain rivulet supplying the water is known among the natives as the "Altmhengan," or "the burn of the bear." When in flood the scene, as the foaming waters dash fiercely over 100 feet of almost perpendicular rock, is an imposing one.

Up the mountain side, a distance of $2\frac{1}{2}$ miles from the village, at an elevation of 1200 feet, are the famed *Aberfoyle Slate Quarries*, where about a hundred workmen are employed by the limited company. The slates, largely in demand for better class work, are conveyed to the railway station by a tramway 2 feet $4\frac{1}{2}$ inch gauge. To a certain point the line is single and the waggons drawn by horses, but for 700 yards the line is double, and descends the face of the steep shoulder of Craigmore. The double portion is self-acting, the loaded waggons going down bringing up the empty ones. During the ascent of this road the view of the valleys of the Forth and Endrick is extensive. After traversing about $3\frac{1}{2}$ miles, *Loch Drunkie* comes in sight on the right.

In making the descent toward Loch Achray, one of the finest panoramas is revealed. On the left is the dark Ben Venue (2393 feet), Loch Katrine, the source of Glasgow's water supply, and Ben A'n; in the front Glen Finlas, and to the east Ben Ledi (2875 feet), the combination of mountain, wood, dale, and water producing a "scene of unspeakable grandeur and beauty."

The nearer view of the Trossachs from the heights

TROSSACHS PIER, LOCH KATRINE.

above Loch Achray is most enchanting. Our first impression of this scene, strengthened no doubt by associations with that fairest creation of Sir Walter Scott—"The Lady of the Lake"—has never been effaced, although it happened before our good friend Macadam had visited the region, or the scream of the locomotive had been heard.

After joining the Trossachs Road at the west side of Loch Achray, a short distance to the right is the Trossachs Hotel. To the left is the *Pass of the Trossachs*, where winds the path to Loch Katrine, a mile distant. The sail up the Loch to Stronachlachar, *en route* for Loch Lomond, is delightful. The surface of the loch, flecked by touches of sun and clouds, the mountains around reflected in its transparent waters, and Ellen's Isle, in sylvan apparel, the home of the fair "Lady of the Lake," form a picture which, once looked upon, will be for ever remembered.

A mile along the shore from the pier is the *Silver Strand*, near which is Ellen's Isle.

Popular Drives and Walks to Scenes of "The Lady of the Lake" and Romance of "Rob Roy."

1. Old Clachan of Aberfoyle—½ mile.
2. Historic Pass of Aberfoyle, leading up to Loch Ard—1½ miles.
3. The Bailie's Rock and Tree, and famous Cave of Rob Roy—3 miles.

4. Ledard Fall—4½ miles.
5. Lochs Dhu and Chon, "in the birch-grown beauty of the hills"—7 miles.
6. Lake of Menteith, with its island ruins of Inchmahome, famous in Scottish history as the refuge of Queen Mary—5 miles.
7. Lovely Circular Drive by Duchray's Old Castle and Glasgow Corporation Water Works' Aqueduct, and round Loch Ard, commanding magnificent view of the Loch on the route—13½ miles.
8. Circular Drive by Lake of Menteith, Cardross, Arnprior, Buchlyvie, Gartfarran Peel, Flanders Moss, and Gartmore—20 miles.
9. Circular Drive to Trossachs, Callander, and Lake of Menteith—27 miles.
10. Circular Walk by Camahlatair Waterfall, and back by Craigmore, with fine view of the Aberfoyle Valley—1 mile.
11. Lovely Walk to Milton and Duchray Castle—6 miles.
12. Circular Walk by Fairy Knowe and Gartmore Bridge—4 miles.
13. Crags of Ben Venue, Craig More, Craig Vat, and Meull Ear—all in walking distance.
14. Beautiful Drives to—
   Stronachlachar, ... 12 miles.
   Callander, ... 12 miles.
   Inversnaid Falls on Loch Lomond side, 16 miles.
   Stirling Castle, ... 20 miles.

Angling.—Excellent trout fishing is to be had on Lochs Ard and Chon. Boats are let at the Bailie Nicol Jarvie Hotel.

From the Mountain Tops.

NOTWITHSTANDING the various objects of attraction to which the attention of the visitor has been directed, we would strongly recommend him, should his time permit of it, to ascend one or other of the undernoted hilltops, and obtain a bird's eye view of Strathendrick. Few straths in Scotland can be seen to better advantage in this way than this lovely vale, stretching along the north side of the Campsie Fells. The most frequented view point is undoubtedly Ben Lomond, the view to be had on a clear day from the summit of this outer sentinel of the Grampians, is perhaps equal to any in the Kingdom. In making the ascent from Rowardennan, ample opportunities have been afforded of viewing the charming scenery of the loch and its surroundings, so that when the top is reached, the most attractive object is the grand panorama of hills to the north, nearly every hilltop being visible from the Paps of Jura on the west to Ben Nevis on the north, then turning eastwards scarcely less attractive than the other is the uninterrupted view to be had of the valley of the Forth, stretching from Loch Ard onwards past Stirling till broken by the Saline Hills in Fife. After having seen the objects of attraction to the north and east the eye will naturally turn southward and rest upon the fairy grandeur of the loch and its wooded islands, while to the left, beyond the Pass of

Balmaha, lies lower Strathendrick, the wooded policies of Buchanan Castle enriching the scene, and the river, as seen from here, looks like a silver thread as it empties its waters into the Queen of Scottish Lakes.

Although less frequented than Ben Lomond the finest views of Strathendrick are to be had from several points of the Campsie Fells. Of these, the most approachable are Dungoyne (1401 feet), within an hour of the station of the same name, and the Earl's Seat (1894 feet), the highest point of the Campsies, and almost within an hour of Balfron. The view to be had from either of these points on a clear day is quite entrancing, embracing the whole of Strathendrick and the Menteith district of Perthshire onwards to Strathallan, while the Grampian range, from the Cowal Hills in Argyleshire to Ben Lawers, form the background of a picture that once seen will never be forgotten.

Another point of the Campsies that will repay its ascent is the Meikle Bin (1870 feet), approached from the Craw Road between Fintry and Lennoxtown. The attractions here are an equally fine view of the Grampian range, Abbey Craig, and the Ochils from Demyat to Glendevon, with the various towns along their base. On this hill, and the smaller hills surrounding it, three streams take their rise, viz., the Endrick, the Carron, and the Glassart, running through the famous Campsie Glen. Several years ago the following verses, from the pen of the Rev. Jas. Mather, Dalry,. Galloway, appeared in the "United Presbyterian Magazine," and express what this lover of Nature felt on visiting this spot—

"My footsteps sped into a glen
  At foot of Muckle Bin,
Where mossy waters run in haste
  And made a babbling din.

To north they went a little space
  And joined the Carron stream,
While eastward up the hill I bore
  Beneath the noon-day beam.

As often as I turned me back,
  And looked into the west,
Afar the mountains stood in rank
  In azure and at rest.

Ben Lomond o'er his waters dark,
  And o'er his islets green,
And Ben Venue, whose rocky breast
  Shuts in a fairy scene.

Beyond the Trossachs and Ben A'n,
  And north the Finlas Glen,
Ben Ledi reared his triple peak
  O'er Lubnaig's darksome den.

In majesty Ben Voirlich rose
  Above Glen Artney's braes,
And in the breast of fair Loch Earn
  The face of heaven could trace.

Stobinnain o'er Balquhidder stood
  Abreast with high Ben More,
And far to north Ben Lawers broad
  Surveyed the Rannoch Moor.

I knew them well, those mountains old,
  At sight of them arose
The shades of dim and distant years
  As mist where Carron flows.

Before the south and east, the clouds
  O'erhung the Forth and plain,
The sun shot arrows through the gloom,
  A bright and beaming rain.

The Forth was hid, but Abbey Craig
  Before the Ochils stood,
And bore the Wallace Monument
  Above the misty flood.

There may it stand as long as time,
  Or hills that wear the heath,
And let the name of Wallace live
  As long as Scotsmen breathe.

Adown the Bin unto the south
  I crossed the boggy Fell,
From cairn to cairn to Campsie brow,
  And thence into the dell."

. . . .

Dungoyne, the Earl's Seat, and the Meikle Bin are all, comparatively speaking, easy of ascent, the view to be had from the summit of each being such as will amply repay the lover of nature.

Cycling

In and about Strathendrick.

TO the cyclist, actual or prospective, Strathendrick offers advantages possessed by no other district in the peculiar variety it affords the sojourner within its bounds and upon its borders.

It is only a few years since some unknown but intrepid cyclist discovered the district, and made known to the world that there were roads to most of the villages and hamlets, and out of these again. Since then the neighbourhood has advanced in popularity with wheeling people.

Lying equi-distant from Glasgow, Stirling, and Dumbarton, these centres are within easy reach by roads which, all more or less undulating, are very good. From Glasgow a choice of routes is open, that through Milngavie and Strathblane being the most direct and most frequented, while the Drymen Road through Bearsden and over Stockie Muir is a more secluded if stiffer route. Journeying by Campsie, the road is easier if the Strathblane branch be taken, but if preferred the Craw Road over the Campsie Fells leads into the village of Fintry, and beyond it to Kippen, Buchlyvie, Stirling, etc. This road requires push on one side and caution on the other, more than one cyclist having encountered catastrophe for want of the latter.

On the Fintry side it may be as well to admire the scenery dismounting, as the descent is sharp and surprising in places, the last turn being particularly perilous to the unsuspicious stranger who may be apt to experience more bad turns in ten minutes than good ones in ten days. The surface of this road is usually good.

No matter which road may be chosen, the same caution is often necessary. The descent into the valley of the Blane on the Milngavie and Strathblane road includes a nasty bend, which may run one "slap" into a moo-cow or a travelling menagerie, a flock of sheep or a four-in-hand picnic party. The drop into Blanefield is also worth some care, especially when school is "skailing."

On the Drymen road one will find a long, not very stiff, pull up to the summit, with a long run down hill on the other side, but the road is a quiet one and the risks few. The road to Killearn branches off just beyond Finnich Glen, one of the show places of the neighbourhood.

Once within the district, many little-tours may be arranged, devised, and varied infinitely to suit the taste, leisure, and capability of the cyclist, the chiefest charm of all being the variety. To the veriest tyro this is an encouragement and an education, to the expert a joy and delight.

Of one visitor, some years ago, it is recorded that he learned to ride on Monday, compassed 12 miles on Tuesday, 20 on Wednesday, 30 on Thursday, 40 on

BALMAHA PIER, LOCH LOMOND.

Friday, and 50 on Saturday, the points visited in course of this performance including Balmaha, Aberfoyle and Loch Ard; Lake of Menteith, Callander, Doune, and Stirling: not a bad record for a novice by any means.

From Balfron, which we may reckon the centre, it is possible to leave by the north or the south, the east or the west, and to return within the hour from any side, and these circular journeys can easily be extended anywhere between the hour and the day. Northward the road is stiff for a mile, two miles out the Stirling and Dumbarton Road is joined at Kepculloch Toll. Eastward then by Buchlyvie, Arnprior, Kippen, and returning over the hill via Fintry, one may obtain fine, picturesque views of a somewhat remote neighbourhood.

If at Arnprior the turn is taken to the left, a finely-wooded road leads to the beautiful and historically famous Lake of Menteith, unique in Scottish scenery, Scotland's only lake. Here, Thornhill, Doune, and Stirling lie straight away to the right. Aberfoyle and Loch Ard to the left, and following this as our homeward route the road branches again to the left just before Aberfoyle is in view, and leads by Gartmore Station, Ward Toll, and Balfron Station. The perilous spot on this lovely round is the ugly dip between Port of Menteith Station and the Lake, about a mile from the latter. To reach Callander from Menteith, a stiff pull over a rather rough road gains one the summit of the ridge. On the steepest part of the succeeding dip into the valley there is a gate which every good cyclist is expected to open for him-

K

self and close for his successor. This interesting feature of the landscape it will be as well to bear in mind the first time, there being no danger of forgetting it a second time. From Callander Doune may be reached by a splendid road, and thence Stirling via Dunblane or Kincardine, or turning backwards again by Thornhill and Kippen Station the round may be completed.

From Callander the Trossachs are easily reached by the shores of Loch Vennacher and Loch Achray.

A good but very steep road winds upwards over the hill to Aberfoyle. This road is of recent construction, albeit an ancient and honourable custom is still observed in the exaction of toll dues.

From Callander one may find his way into the most picturesque regions of Scotland, and penetrate into the very heart of the Highlands.

Northwards by Loch Lubnaig and Loch Earn to Comrie and Crieff, or via Glenogle to Killin and Loch Tay and Kenmore are splendid routes, while Crianlarich and Loch Lomond offer another which will linger long in the remembrance.

Back to Balfron again, a nice round is by Kepculloch Toll, Drymen, Croftamie, Finnich Toll and Killearn. Beyond Drymen lie Balmaha and Rowardennan (Ben Lomond), but the road on this side of Loch Lomond must not be expected to feel so good as that across the water.

Between Drymen village and its station the road branches to Balloch and Dumbarton, by which route the lonely hills of the west or the busy shores of Clyde are equally accessible.

In another direction, viz., by Strathblane, Campsie, and Milngavie, the runs are pretty, easily compassed and variable at will.

Eastward up the valley lies Fintry, at the junction of the roads to Campsie and Glasgow, Kippen and Stirling, while another and rougher holds onwards up the Endrick, and down the Carron to Carronbridge, where it branches on the right to Kilsyth, on the left to Stirling by Bannockburn. Straight on lie Denny and Falkirk, the road, improving as it goes, forming a pleasant and expeditious route to the East Coast. The other branches afford considerable variety as to surface and gradient, which as often as not adds to the enjoyment of a pleasurable outing when all other conditions are favourable.

The briefest study of a good map will convince anyone of the peculiar geographical advantages, the strategic value, so to speak, of the position from a cycling point of view, and the wheeling visitor who may ramble along the routes of his choice, as this description has, will find much to admire, much to enjoy, much to beware, and lay up a volume of remembrance he will never lose, even although he do not rush every yard of the good macadam to be found on the list and on the map.

THE ENDRICK.

Ah! Endrick, bring me back again the band
That played with me beside thy silver strand;
Such chorus from our hearts and lips would ring,
Would wake thy echoes, rouse thy rocks to sing.

Alas! love cannot call them back again
To sing thy praise, or chant the loud refrain;
But still thy waters rush on to the lake,
Making sweet melody in dell and brake.
And other voices sing their youthful song,
Lay on thy bosom, as thou hurriest along.
Their laughter and their love; as hearts of yore,
Who've crossed the bar and reached the heavenly shore.

Roll on, sweet river, pure and undefiled!
Tell every stalwart youth and maiden mild
To live like thee, unstained and good—
By faith in Him who died on holy rood.
Sing them thy song of gladness and of joy;
Win them in youth, and teach them to employ
Their strength, their will, their hearts, their pen
In praise of God and love to brother men.
Sweet Endrick! river of my first delight,
Forgive this song, I've sung before the night,
Seal the poor singer's lips and hide his face
From thee and all from whom he begs one last embrace!

J. W. K.

Angling.

Some Hints by an Angler.

THE Endrick, rising in the heights east of Fintry, and flowing into Loch Lomond near Balmaha, is a good example of a trout stream. The water is fairly rapid for the most part, and, flowing over rocks and gravel, it is normally clear, except for a slightly reddish tinge due to iron. As it nears the Loch it becomes more sluggish, and the pools are deeper.

Being connected with the sea by Loch Lomond and the River Leven, it is favoured in the early autumn with the presence of sea trout and salmon, which ascend the river when the water is in favourable condition, and the angler on the spot may expect to get a sea trout at least. There are pike in the lower parts of the river, but, for angling purposes, the principal fish are yellow trout. These are not huge, reaching a weight of a pound, or occasionally two pounds, but they are the exception, and over a season's fishing they may be taken to scale five or six to the pound. The quality, however, in the season is irreproachable. The Endrick trout is not by any means a guileless creature. On the contrary it seems to have gone in for higher education, and benefited thereby. The youth one hears of who fishes with a line of ham twine and bent pin attachment will find himself very far out if he seeks profitable sport in Endrick.

Other things being equal, the angler with the fine tackle will have most to show at weighing time. Though angling cannot be learned from books, a few hints may be useful, and such as given have been tried and proved serviceable. The time when Endrick trout are in season may be put at from March till September, and they are not worth taking earlier or later than these months, as the stream is a late one.

The best lures are fly, worm, and minnow. The flies are of no special kind. They should be on a No. 14 hook for day fishing, and a No. 12 or 11 for night work. If the angler has, say two dozen varieties of quiet-coloured flies, he has all he needs. These may be black, grey, and brown hackles to represent spiders; and teal, woodcock, pheasant, and partridge, with a few shades of dun, such as may be obtained from the starling's or lark's wing. The bodies may vary, and may be formed of hare-lug, quill or silk, yellow being a good colour and a favourite.

The night flies for June, July, and August may be the zulu, a black hackle with red tip, the corncrake, and the coachman, a white winged fly. The maggot or gentle is often an extra inducement for either day or night fishing, though, by some, it is considered unsportsmanlike to use it on a fly.

In working the fly, whether by day or night, it is most deadly if cast so as to appear as if it had dropped off the bank. Some of the larger-sized evening flies found on the banks and stuck on a small hook sometimes prove deadly.

The Minnow.—This, if natural, is a good bait, and may be fresh or salted, though the former is the better.

They should be small, say 1½ inches, and mounted on a small spinner, which makes them more attractive, because more life-like. When the stream is larger than usual, a larger minnow can be used, and if the colour of the salted minnows be good they may do very well, as trout do not object to a little seasoning in their food. Trout seem to follow a minnow for the purpose of smelling it, and they very often seize it just where the water is getting so shallow that the angler is thinking of making a fresh cast, though, on the other hand, it may be very quickly seized.

The most killing bait for any state of the water is the worm. It does best in bright, cloudless weather whether the water be big or little. For brown or discoloured water worms are best freshly dug out of the garden or manure heap. The trout have then the sense of smell to help that of sight, which is necessarily not so keen in that state of the water. Their taste, too, at such a time is clearly proved to be most catholic, as is seen when the angler, in unhooking his victim, often gets a handful of winged and creeping creatures of all sorts out of the fish's mouth.

In fishing the Endrick when the water is clear, the worms should be small, say, two inches long, on a small Stewart tackle on fine gut. The worms are the better for a day or two in moss to toughen and enliven them. When the water is small fishing up stream is necessary to avoid disturbing the fish, which, of course, are then looking away from the angler.

In bright, sunny weather, when the water is so small that the fish are confined to the pools, these may be worked from the lower end wading slowly and gently up, casting right in front, and using only a small pellet for a sinker. If there be also a little wind to ruffle the surface the angler will be astonished perhaps to discover how many fine fish he has got to redeem his time, for this method of fishing will profit him when no other will. The fishing may also be done from the bank if there are bushes to conceal the fisher, but it is trying work then, and somewhat resembles deer-stalking. Sometimes, too, in the heat of summer, when the fly seems of no use, trout may be got with the worm in the shallows if there be a breeze and the angler use a long-line and fish up stream. Trout, and big ones, too, leave their haunts, then, and come out to feed just as they do at night.

Certain fastidious persons object to worm fishing as unsportsmanlike, but they certainly have not tried clear water worming or pool fishing when the water was very small, or they would be obliged to confess that the angler had to work hard for his reward. Of course it is true that worm fishing in brown water does not require great skill, but the country lad at such times only has a chance of adding trout to his menu, as his tackle is not often fine enough or so varied as to afford him much hope of success when streams are low and limpid. Much may be forgiven him and the mere tyro therefore, for the latter may in time, if the fates prove kind, so increase in skill as to be able to turn up his nose with the most sportsmanlike at whatsoever is not considered quite the correct thing in angling.

Some Geological Features of Strathendrick.

THE Strath is bounded on the south by the Campsie Fells, which evidently form the barrier line between the carboniferous strata on the southern side and the Old Red Sandstone constituting, with its surface conglomerates, the rock-bed on the Strathendrick face.

These hills are evidently of volcanic formation, partly by upheaval and partly by trap accumulation, but it is a matter of conjecture only whether this trap be a dyke-flow from some central crater or series of craters, or otherwise a solid wedge forced upward through the superincumbent strata.

The period of such upheaval and volcanic overflow provides an interesting subject of study, and if we can find a rock stratum apparently continuous on both sides of the Fells we may reasonably conclude that it has been covered by the overflowing trap, or torn up by volcanic energy. In either case the stratum must have been earlier than the trap, its age should indicate the eruptive period, and some evidence on this point is attainable.

At the Mount Quarry on Ballikinrain there is an

outcrop, from the direction of the hills, of white millstone grit, a seam traceable westwards on the estate, and evidently that which is worked at the Duke's Quarries above Killearn. Its continuation towards Strathblane is problematic, but around the north-west and south side of the hills its elevation is apparently constant, and it seems to have been either rent asunder, or submerged by the fluid trap.

The millstone grit, overlying the mountain limestone, is the second lowest of the carboniferous strata; the Old Red Sandstone, older still, is classed among the highest or most modern of the primary (not primitive) rocks.

Another interesting problem is presented by the Park Quarry, where the removal of the trap has exposed the contiguous sandstone conglomerates overlying the Old Devonian, which break off in strata more or less horizontal, with a vertical lining of limestone.

Considering the proportional dimensions of the rift, it seems improbable that the trap had been forced up from below, and the trend of the fissure and the ridge stretching away eastward nearly to the Gargunnock Hills by Balgair and Kippen, where limestone abounds, suggests the idea of a great volcanic crater in that direction pouring forth its molten flood, whose superficial flux of limestone settled into and occupied the spaces occasioned by the cooling and solidification of the mass.

Finnich Glen is a fine example of the abrasive action of running water, although we may only guess to what extent this and similar glens are indebted to that action alone; but that the Carnock has so enormously deepened its rocky bed is apparent, and decisive evidence of the immensity of that period which has elapsed since the Old Red Sandstone became the dry land, and since any appreciable alteration of the contour of the district has taken place.

Similar evidence proving that our coal beds were formed ages before such streams began to flow upon the surface, or in the fissures of the rock, we begin in some measure to realise the significance of the phrase, "Period of geological formation."

The Whangie is another and perhaps a better illustration of rock abrasion and earth rupture.

In the Fintry gorge, on the Endrick, are many indications of the tailing-off of the coal and lime formations.

From the neighbourhood of Buchlyvie eastward there are all the evidences of the existence of an ancient channel or estuary, the fertile levels of the carse of Stirling having been undoubtedly formed by the gradual silting up of the tideway. Westwards the land is undulating, its contour being clearly due to subterraneous volcanic waves, and numerous instances are to be found of violent rock rupture and dislocation of strata in every possible angle.

To the student this district must be almost fallow ground, and the seeing eye and the thoughtful mind may possibly discover, in addition to the marine crustacea commonly found in the sandstones, other and hitherto undiscerned links in the history of this surface crust, which, so firm, is yet so fragile when compared with the tremendous bulk of the molten mass contained and concealed within its fiery interior.

Botanical Notes.

THIS district, it may be asserted, is equalled by few other districts in Scotland, and surpassed by none, as a happy hunting-ground for the lover of wild-flowers. The reason of this is to be found in the charming variety of the landscape: hill and dale, moorland and lea, intersected by a net-work of rivulets, hastening on "to join the brimming river."

Practically all classes of inland wild flowers, whether their habitation be the breezy moor or the dusty roadside; the woodland glade or the river bank, are to be found in rich profusion.

Thus, in trudging over the moors, we come across such characteristic specimens as Scabious (Scabiosa succisa), Tormentil (Potentilla tormentilla), Milkwort (Polygala vulgaris), Butterwort (Pinguicula vulgaris), Bog Asphodel (Narthecium ossifragum), with many another flower which is "born to blush unseen, and waste its sweetness on the desert air."

In the fields we find the Pink Persicaria (Polygonum persicaria), Corn Marigold (Chrysanthemum segetum), Wild Pansy (Viola tricolor), Scarlet Pimpernel (Anagallis arvensis), White and Red Dead Nettle (Laminium album and L. purpureum), some of which varieties are not held in particularly high esteem by the farmers.

Then in the pastures we shall not fail to perceive Selfheal (Prunella vulgaris), Eyebright (Euphrasia officinalis), Lady's Smock (Cardamine pratensis), Ragwort (Senecio jacobæa). When tired of the open ground we make a sally into the woods "Adown whose scented banks the cushat croodles am'rously," and discover in their cool retreat Cow Wheat (Melampyrum pratense), Anemone (Anemone nemorosa), Woodsorrel (Oxalis acetosella), Woodruff (Asperula odorata), Hyacinth (Agraphis nutans), the last named of which bedeck the woods in the springtime with a mantle of blue, and by their sweet perfume tell the wanderer of their presence long before his eyes contemplate the fairy scene.

After all, it is near the water that a visitor from the smoky city loves to linger, to listen to the voice of the stream as it brawls down the glen, leaping from rock to rock in miniature cascades, and splashing gleefully the flowerets standing expectant upon the bank to catch the drops which fall like diamonds to adorn their brows. It is in such spots as these that we find the Lesser Celandine (Ranunculus ficaria), Ragged Robin (Lychnis flos-cuculi), Red Campion (Lychnis diurna), Valerian (Valeriana officinalis).

But it is perhaps on the waysides and in the hedgerows that we find the greatest assemblage of wild flowers, Nature, who abhors a vacuum, having clothed these waste places in garments surpassing fair. Here we see a mass of Speedwell (Veronica chamædrys), whose pure deep blue is agreeably varied by the pale star-like flowers of the Stitchwort (Stellaria holostea) and the delicate milk-white sprays of the Bedstraw (Gallium mollugo). Among the dust at the roadside we find the Restharrow (Ononis arvensis) and the Silverweed (Potentilla anserina); and in the hedges the Honeysuckle (Lonicera periclymenum) and the Wild Rose (Rosa canina).

There is something peculiarly fascinating about ferns. They are devoid of gay colours, but the sober green and graceful outline and disposition of parts make them pleasing, and give to them a singular beauty. The varieties to be found in the district are numerous, and include—Common Polypody (Polypodium vulgare), Beech Fern (Polypodium phegopteris), Oak Fern (Polypodium dryopteris), Mountain Parsley (Allosorus crispus), Prickly Shield (Polystichum aculeatum), Mountain Buckler (Lastrea Montana), Male Fern (Lastrea filix-mas), Lady Fern (Athyrium filix foemina), Wall Rue (Asplenium ruta muraria), Green Spleenwort (Asplenium viride), Common Maidenhair Spleenwort (Asplenium trichomanes), Common Hart's Tongue (Scolopendrium vulgare). The list might be lengthened, the writer in his expeditions having come across many others, and it would be easy to fill page after page in this wise. Suffice it to say that to him who knows and loves the wild-flowers there is an added charm in the landscape; and as he wends his way along the dusty highway, or turns aside into the refreshing coolness of some sequestered dell, he is everywhere greeted by some floweret sweet, that, looking trustfully up, awakens in him happy memories of bygone days. For flowers were not made merely to be dissected and baptised with high-sounding Latin names: they were created "to minister delight to man and beautify the earth."

> And with childlike, credulous affection,
> We behold their tender buds expand;
> Emblems of our own great resurrection,
> Emblems of the bright and better land.

But whether he be botanist, poet, painter, or simple lover of Nature for her own sake, he will find endless variety, endless grace and beauty in the wild-flowers and ferns of this picturesque and interesting region.

Farming in Strathendrick.

THIS being a purely agricultural district, a guide-book would not be complete without a reference to the system of farming in practice.

Soil.—The general character of the soil along the Strath is that of a sandy loam, derived from the old Red Sandstone. There are stretches also of stiff argillaceous soils and of alluvial deposits.

Cropping.—On the majority of farms the crops are raised, not for sale, but for home consumption, the feeding of stock for sale and dairy purposes.

The rotation generally followed is:—First year, oats; second, green crop; third, oats; fourth, seeds mown; after which it lies in grass, two, three, or four years, but more frequently three. Lea oats usually receive from 2 to 3 cwts. of superphosphate and about 1 cwt. of sulphate of ammonia or nitrate of soda. On well farmed lands, the red-land gets a dressing of from 3 to 4 cwts. of bone meal or flour, according to the texture of the land. The varieties sown are Providence, Hamilton, Long Houghton, Tam Finlay, or Sandy, the latter being the predominating variety for red-land. The average yield per imperial acre is 32 bushels, weighing from 36 to 42 lbs., and selling about 15s. a boll, the straw per acre being about 30 cwts, and worth about £2 10s. per ton. Green crop embraces

LOCH ARD, ABERFOYLE.

turnips, potatoes, and cabbages. This is the crop that receives all the manure made on the holdings in the preceding year, and it is during its preparation for this and the working of the growing crop that the land is cleaned. In addition to farmyard manure, the crop usually receives about 3 cwts. of a general artificial manure, the phosphates, potash or ammonia predominating as the farmer deems necessary.

Turnips are grown in drills about 27 inches wide, giving an average of 15 tons per acre, yellow turnips realizing about 10s. per ton and swedes about 16s.

Potatoes are planted in drills about 29 inches wide, and produce from 5 to 6 tons per imperial acre, but on good potato land a crop of 10 tons is attainable. The price of potatoes varies considerably, the custom in the strath being to sell them by the imperial acre, and an average price is about £13, although sometimes a half more than that is received.

Cabbages are grown only to a very limited extent, the few who do cultivate them raising about 30 tons on the single acre planted for the use of the dairy cows and sheep.

The predominating grass or clover in the hay crop are Italian ryegrass and red clover. Other grasses and clovers are sown, such as Perennial Ryegrass, Meadow Fescue, Timothy, Cocksfoot, Meadow Foxtail, White, and Alsike Clovers, but they do not show up very well the first year, their herbage being more conspicuous in the following grazing years. An average crop of hay is about 35 cwts. per acre, worth about £3 per ton. It is usually top-dressed with about 3 cwts. of a general manure.

There is another rotation practised in the strath which may be termed the "Boulder Clay Rotation," and followed on that class of soil where green cropping is unprofitable, owing to its stiffness. This soil extends from the west side of Ballikinrain estate to Gartness, and strikes south along the Valley of the Blane to Duntreath, and the crops taken are—First year, oats; second, mashlem, receiving the farmyard manure; third, oats again; fourth year, seeds mown, thereafter grazed. By this rotation, as the land has a tendency to get foul, every alternate rotation is summer fallowed in place of mashlem. Some farmers find it profitable to have a few acres sown down with Timothy, as it gives a good crop, useful for all kinds of stock. The treatment generally given is 15 tons of farmyard manure to the acre one year, and the next a mixture consisting of 1 cwt. sulphate of ammonia, 1 cwt. bone meal, and 2 cwts. superphosphate.

Cattle.—The cattle bred or reared in the district are chiefly Ayrshires. Some farmers cross with a Polled-Angus bull and some with the Shorthorn. The pure bred Ayrshires are all reared for milk production, while the crosses are sold as stores or fed off. The milk is utilized in rearing calves, making butter and cheese, or retailed in the neighbourhood, or sent from the nearest railway station to Glasgow. The average price of milk sent by rail is $6\frac{3}{4}$d. per gallon, delivered in Glasgow, the local retail price at the cart 10d.

A few churn all their milk, and sell the butter and butter-milk in the neighbourhood at an average of 1s per lb. for butter and 2d. per gallon for butter-milk. The kind of cheese made is principally cheddar, which, after being thoroughly ripened, is sold to merchants for about 56s. per cwt.

The price of good young calving cows varies from £12 to £16; queys from £10 to £12; two-year-old yield queys when sold realize from £7 to £8, and stirks about £5. Two-year-old Ayrshire store bullocks delivered at the 1st of May bring from £6 to £9. Prime fat cattle fetch about 36s. per cwt. live weight, lighter kinds, not so well finished, 2s. or 3s. less.

Horses.—The favourite horse is of course the Clydesdale. There are no breeding establishments in the Strath, but most farmers keep a good work mare for the further purpose of keeping up his stock. Two-year-olds bring about £30, while well-seasoned work horses command about £45.

Sheep.—The principal breed of sheep is the blackface; a few breed Leicesters, while some breed from Cheviots and half-breds; nearly all the blackfaced stocks are crossed with Border Leicester tups, the lambs realizing in August from 18s. to 22s.

There are some very pure and famous stocks of blackfaces in the Strath, a trade amongst them being the bringing out of shearling rams, and those will average about £5 each when sold in September. As an illustration of the interest taken in this department of agriculture in this district, Mr. J. C. Dun-Waters, late of Craigton, paid in September, 1896, £135 for a shearling ram out of Mr. Howatson's Glenbuck stock at Perth sales, a record price for this class of sheep. The cast ewes realize from 18s. to 22s., and blackfaced hoggs, when bought to maintain the stock, cost about 18s. An average price for blackface wool is about 5d. per lb., while other sorts bring about 6d. per lb.

Pigs.—Pig breeding or rearing is not practised to any great extent; suffice it to say that some of the farmers keep a sow, the produce of which is sold when five or six weeks old for about 16s. each, and well fed pigs, not too heavy, bring about 52s. per cwt. dead weight.

Poultry.—This department of farm work is relegated to the women folks, and in some instances is conducted with intelligence and success. The number of fowls kept about a farmhouse varies from 50 to 100, consisting for the most part of first crosses, and the best known breeds of what are regarded as utility birds, Minorcas and the various families of Leghorns, especially white, predominating. The class of poultry has greatly improved during the last few years. In hatching and rearing, while most adhere to the natural method by means of hens, a few have adopted incubators and foster mothers. Fowls are kept primarily for eggs, which are sold to shops at from 9d. to 1s. 8d. per dozen according to the season, or an average of 1s. per dozen over the year.

THE END.

ADVERTISEMENTS.

TELEPHONES—　　　　　　　　　　　　　　　　TELEGRAPHIC ADDRESS—
National, - 2502.　　**ESTABLISHED 1851.**　　"KELLY,
Corporation, Y250.　　　　　　　　　　　　　　　PARKHEAD,
　　　　　　　　　　　　　　　　　　　　　　　GLASGOW."

J. H. KELLY,

Cart, Van, and Lorry Builder,

PARKHEAD, GLASGOW.

BUILDER OF ALL KINDS OF

Milk Vans.	Hay Waggons.
Milk Carts.	Cattle Floats.
Chapel Carts.	Garden Barrows.
Farm Carts.	Grocers' Barrows.
	&c., &c.

PRICES ON APPLICATION.

☞ Wheels re-rung and Loose Tyres tightened by Hydraulic Process. Done while you wait.

Pianofortes for Hire.

VISITORS to the COAST, HIGHLANDS, SOUTH and WESTERN DISTRICTS OF SCOTLAND, can very conveniently be supplied with PIANOFORTES, &c., on Hire at the minimum of expense from the Establishments of

PATERSON, SONS & CO.,
152 Buchanan Street, GLASGOW;

Gilmour Street, PAISLEY; 34 Newmarket Street, AYR; 81 King Street, KILMARNOCK; 20 English Street, DUMFRIES; 23 West Blackhall Street, GREENOCK.

The Oldest Established and Most Complete Wholesale News-Agency in Scotland.

Established 1837.   Telephone, No. 4822.

WILLIAM LOVE,
Wholesale News=agent, Bookseller, and Stationer,
219a and 221 ARGYLE STREET,
(Opposite Central Station),

GLASGOW.

WE supply the trade with NEWSPAPERS, PERIODICALS, MAGAZINES, BOOKS, and STATIONERY at best terms and with the utmost despatch.

STATIONERY SHOW ROOM with a splendid range of Samples of General Stationery at 219a and 221 Argyle Street, opposite Caledonian Railway Central Station.

Lists and Prices sent free to any Country Agent or Store-Keeper.

ADVERTISEMENTS.

JAMES PATON,

Registered Plumber,

Buchanan Street,
BALFRON.

ESTIMATES

Furnished for every kind of SANITARY, HEATING, and HYDRAULIC WORK.

Repairs Promptly Executed.

Telegraphic Address—"PATON, PLUMBER, BALFRON."

ADVERTISEMENTS.

NEIL MACKAY,
ROPE AND TWINE MANUFACTURER
CITY ROPERIE,
66 WEST HOWARD STREET,

Telephone, 3354 (Royal).
Established 1879.

GLASGOW.

LEADING CONTRACTOR TO AGRICULTURISTS IN SCOTLAND.

Sole maker of the featherweight scaffold ropes and plumbers' tackles, made from the finest hand spun tarred bolt rope, pliable in all weathers, fitted complete with patent roller sheaved safety iron stroped Blocks, and latest safety Improvements, in view of Employers' Liability Act. Hundreds of sets have been sold.

GARDEN NETS—ROPES, TWINES, AND LINES FOR ALL PURPOSES.

GOODS DELIVERED in City or Suburbs, or Carefully Packed for Coast or Country, FREE OF CHARGE.

JOHN ARBUCKLE,
WHOLESALE AND RETAIL
GLASS AND CHINA MERCHANT,

488 SAUCHIEHALL STREET, | **457 GREAT WESTERN ROAD,**
Near Charing Cross, and | Caledonia Mansions, Kelvin Bridge,

GLASGOW,

Where he keeps a large and varied stock of the best makes, at very moderate prices.

At 488 SAUCHIEHALL STREET, the flat above is kept exclusively for odd and job lots of all kinds of useful, ornamental, and faulty goods at job prices.

SPECIAL TERMS GIVEN TO HOTELS, RESTAURANTS, &c.

INSPECTION INVITED.

MAKERS OF
LOZENGES, PAN GOODS, MIXTURES, GUM, ITALIAN GUM, GELATINE, BOILED SUGAR GOODS.

Cut Rocks & Tablets Specialities.

W. & J. M'LINTOCK,
DUNMORE STREET & Glasgow,
M'NEILL STREET,
WHOLESALE AND EXPORT MANUFACTURERS OF
JAMS, JELLIES, MARMALADES,
and CONFECTIONERY.

ESTABLISHED 1869.

NATIONAL—249 Gorbals.

All Grocers and Confectioners will consult their own and Customers' interests by Stocking our Goods.

JAM FACTORY—
OATLANDS, LANARKSHIRE.

ADVERTISEMENTS.

WILLIAM BUCHANAN,

JOINER AND CONTRACTOR,

3 DALHOUSIE STREET,

OFF SAUCHIEHALL STREET,

GLASGOW.

ESTIMATES GIVEN.   JOBBINGS PROMPTLY ATTENDED TO.

House—100 BUCCLEUCH STREET.

NATIONAL TELEPHONE, No. 405 (Douglas Exchange).

THE PEOPLE'S JOURNAL
HANDBOOKS
FOR THE PEOPLE.

Handybook of Personal and Household Information (new edition).
Poultry Book (new edition).
Cookery Book.
Knitting and Crochet Book.
Law Book (Scots Law).
Gardening Book.
Dressmaking Book.
Draughts Book.

Mothers' Guide.
Etiquette Book.
Household Guide.
Home Pets.
400 Good Stories.
How to Read, Write, & Debate.
Home Work or Knitting—Book No. 2.
The Cricket Handbook for 1902 (96 pages).
Dog Book.

Aunt Kate's Almanac (annually). The Football Handbook (annually).

40 to 48 pages each—ONE PENNY—of all Newsagents.

ADVERTISEMENTS.

W. & J. BOWIE,

Dyers and French Cleaners,
Carpet Beaters and Renovaters,

CLYDE DYE WORKS,

STRATHCLYDE STREET,

Bridgeton, Glasgow.

PATENTEES AND PROPRIETORS OF STEAM POWER CARPET BEATING AND CARPET CLEANING MACHINERY.

JAMES WALKER,

PAINTER, PAPERHANGER, AND SIGN WRITER,

Buchanan Street, BALFRON.

SELECTION OF PAPERHANGINGS IN STOCK.

PATTERN BOOKS SENT ON APPROVAL.

PAINTS MIXED TO ANY SHADE.

Estimates given for Different Classes of Work.

GRAINING.

ADVERTISEMENTS.

JOHN BUCHANAN,

FAMILY BUTCHER,

204 New City Road,

~~ GLASGOW.

CORNED BEEF AND PICKLED TONGUES.

ROUNDS OF BEEF AND BEEF HAMS.

COLLOPS AND SAUSAGES—A SPECIALITY.

ADVERTISEMENTS.

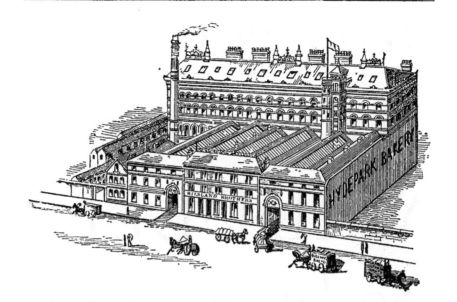

Bilsland's Bread.

Manufactured on the most approved principles of fermentation, from a careful selection of the Choicest

HOME-MADE AND FOREIGN FLOURS.

Retains its full flavour and moistness for a GREAT LENGTH OF TIME.

Sold by Retailers of Bread in all parts of the City and Suburbs, and in various Country Districts.

Hydepark Bakery, Glasgow.

ADVERTISEMENTS.

When in Glasgow

DINE AT
WADDELL'S
60 Union Street.

CENTRAL AND COMMODIOUS.

Moderate Charges.

CITY COMMERCIAL RESTAURANT CO., Ltd.

ADVERTISEMENTS.

A. & C. Mackenzie,
COOPERS,
18a MAINS STREET,
Off ARGYLE STREET,

Glasgow.

STOCK CASKS—
ROUND and OVAL, all Sizes.

SHIP COOPERAGE—
HARNESS CASKS, DECK BUCKETS, OVAL BOATS' BREAKERS, DECK TUBS, Etc.

DAIRY COOPERAGE—
MILK BUTTS and BARRELS, CHURNS, and other Dairy Requisites.

INSPECTION INVITED.

Articles of the Craft made to any desired Design.

ON ADMIRALTY LIST.

ADVERTISEMENTS.

"FACTS ARE CHIELS THAT WINNA DING!"

✠ EVERY MAN ✠
WHO WISHES TO
PRESERVE HIS HEALTH AND PROLONG HIS LIFE
WHILST
PROVIDING AGAINST SICKNESS AND DEATH
Should read the following remarkable evidence from

The Independent Order of Rechabites.

THE testimony of this Order is valuable, because it is a
TEETOTAL BENEFIT SOCIETY
of more than **Sixty years' standing;** it has Branches all over the United Kingdom; and its membership numbers nearly **174,000 Adults** and **104,000 Juveniles,** while its ACCUMULATED FUNDS amount to over **£1,210,000.**

The experience of this large and steadily increasing Society proves most conclusively that, at all periods of adult life, **Abstainers have a substantial advantage** in length of life over users of alcohol.

The following interesting comparison is based upon the Rechabites' mortality experience, as calculated by Mr. F. G. P. NEISON, the eminent Actuary; the mortality of all males, according to the Registrar-General's Report; and the mortality of the well-to-do class whose lives are insured, as estimated by the Institute of Actuaries, and shows that:—

At age 18 all Males have an expectancy of life of **41¾** years.
At age 18 Healthy Males of the well-to-do class have an expectancy of life of .. .. .. } **43½** years.
At age 18 Rechabites have an expectancy of life of **50¼** years.

In other words, the **Teetotal Rechabite** at 18 years of age has an advantage in life expectancy over all Males of 8¾ years, and over Healthy Males of the well-to-do class of 7 years.

These are **Facts worth knowing** and **unassailable.**
Every year's experience confirms their accuracy.
It will be to **your advantage** to abstain. Do it! Join the Rechabite Order, and thus **preserve** your **health** and **prolong** your **life.**

MEMBERSHIP IN SCOTLAND.
In Scotland there are 27,438 Adults, 16,733 Juveniles, 900 Honorary Members, and 1,500 Wives of Members, making a total of 46,571 Members, with funds amounting to over £60,000 sterling.

BENEFITS.
The Funeral and Sickness Benefits range from **5/-** per week during Sickness and **£5** at Death, to **£1** per week during Sickness and **£30** at Death.

CONTRIBUTIONS.
The Monthly Payments range from **3d.** for **2/6** of Sick Allowance at age **15** to **6d.** at age **46,** and **1½d.** for every **£5** Funeral Allowance between **15** and **30,** to **3½d.** between **46** and **50.** Management and Medical Contributions extra.

FORMATION OF A RECHABITE TENT.
Any person desirous of forming a Rechabite Tent should procure an "Application Sheet," on which to get the signatures of ten abstainers or others willing to sign the pledge. The age of candidates must be over 15 and under 50 years. A medical certificate of health must be produced, and an Entrance Fee of 2/6 paid by each candidate.

Application Sheet and fuller particulars may be obtained from

R. D. DUNNACHIE, P.H.C.R., *District Secretary.*

Glasgow District Registered Office: 75 BUCHANAN ST., GLASGOW.